THE GREATEST FRAUD NEVER TOLD

False Accusations, Phony Grand Jury Reports,
and the Assault on the Catholic Church

DAVID F. PIERRE, JR.

TheMediaReport.com : Mattapoisett, Massachusetts

CONTENTS

	Introduction	1
1	"I am an Innocent Man"	5
2	A Lesson From Pope Francis	17
3	The Luck of the Irish	21
4	The Truth About False Accusations	27
5	A Grand Fraud in Pennsylvania	33
6	Pennsylvania Perjury	41
7	Nowhere To Be Found	49
8	A Dangerous Practice	61
9	Buffalo Bias	75
10	The Story Behind the Story in Buffalo	85
11	When the Truth Is Also Victimized	91
12	The Catholic ATM	95
13	A Priest Fights Back	101
14	SNAP Uncovered	105
15	Other Phony Attacks on the Church	113
16	Injustice Down Under	127
17	Dallas Debacle?	133
18	A Call to the Gospel	141
	Index	149
	Also by David F. Pierre, Jr.	153

Introduction

The damage is incalculable.

No discussion related to the topic of Catholic sex abuse can begin without first acknowledging the profound harm wreaked upon victims by criminal priests. John Geoghan, Gilbert Gauthe, Rudy Kos, Ronald Paquin ... they are the names of men who never should have been admitted into a seminary, not to mention the priesthood.

Sex abuse committed by priests were foremost ruinous to the souls of the poor victims. And the damage to the Catholic Church will continue to reverberate for years.

In the mid-1980s, victims began to come forward publicly with excruciating stories of sex abuse committed by priests, and there is little question that the large majority of these cases were indeed true.

These facts are undeniable.

Many decades later, however, there is a new narrative to be told in the "Catholic Church sex abuse story." They are not the reports of angering sex abuse by priests. Rather, they are countless stories of fraud.

THE GREATEST FRAUD NEVER TOLD

Whereas the Church's riches were once offered as a form of restitution to those who were so wounded by clergy, this same money has now become an opportunity for fraudsters, flimflammers, and troubled individuals to score a monetary settlement. This is a bold statement, but the aim of this book is to demonstrate just this.

When a man came forward in 2019 to accuse Diocese of Charleston Bishop Robert Guglielmone of sexually abusing him "between 20 and 30 times from 1978 to 1979," the man openly admitted to a family member that he made the whole thing up in order to score some money. "It's worth a try," he said.[1]

Many others have come to believe that there is nothing to lose in making an abuse claim against a priest and suing the Catholic Church. "It's worth a try." Indeed.

On a Monday morning in 2013, two young men, both in their early twenties, walked into the sacristy of St. Michael Archangel Church in South Chicago after morning Mass. One of the men approached a weak 73-year-old priest and demanded money. He poked the priest in the forehead with his finger and threatened him physically. He then accompanied his threat with an ominous warning:

"We'll say you touched us, read the paper, they'll believe us."[2]

Those young men knew exactly what they were talking about when they said, "They'll believe us." Their words are perfectly indicative of the mindset that has taken hold over the last three decades. No matter how outlandish the claim, no matter how incredible the accusation, the media will dutifully report nearly all claims as if they are unquestionably true. And this important truth has had tragic repercussions.

Introduction

In the wake of the 2018 Pennsylvania grand jury report that made headlines around the world, a newspaper reporter in Florida relayed the astounding claim of a 66-year-old Pennsylvania woman that a priest "began molesting her when she was 9 years old and the abuse continued until she was in her 40s."[3] It was a remarkable accusation, for sure; that she was abused for over three decades.

But the priest's attorney emailed the reporter to politely inform her that if the Pennsylvania woman's abuse had indeed started when she was 9 years old, the priest himself would have been only 16 years old and still in his sophomore and junior years at a high school in Queens, New York. Like so many others, the accuser was clearly a troubled person. A dozen years earlier she had accused a priest of raping her at gunpoint two different times years apart. She had also accused the same priest of "ritual abuse" over a period of seven years at a seminary.[4]

The reporter replied to the attorney saying that she would "update" her story. She never did. Today when readers search for that priest's name on the Internet, they will continue to read of this woman's absurd claim as if it were true.

And what continues is *The Greatest Fraud Never Told.*

NOTES

[1] Josh Berry, "Head of Catholic Church in SC calls sexual abuse allegations 'provably false'." WOLO-TV (ABC affiliate, Columbia, South Carolina), August 14, 2019.
https://www.abccolumbia.com/2019/08/14/head-of-catholic-church-In-sc-calls-sexual-abuse-allegations-provably-false/

[2] Steve Schmadeke and Rosemary Regina Sobel, "2 charged with threatening priest in office, church," *Chicago Tribune*, November 11, 2013. https://www.chicagotribune.com/news/breaking/chi-chicago-crime-south-side-robbery-20131110-story.html

[3] Jane Musgrave, "Priest who worked in Boca accused of abuse by Pennsylvania grand jury," *The Palm Beach Post*, August 16, 2018, https://www.palmbeachpost.com/news/crime--law/priest-who-worked-boca-accused-abuse-pennsylvania-grand-jury/ALwOr2YvnPW35Df3wVglJN/

[4] Matt Abbott, "Woman, Priest Say Abuser Still in Public Ministry," RenewAmerica.com, July 1, 2006.

1

"I am an Innocent Man"

On the night of November 13, 2014, in a prison cell at
the State Correctional Institution in Coal Township,
Pennsylvania, an imprisoned 67-year-old Catholic priest by
the name of Rev. Charles Engelhardt turned to his cellmate,
70-year-old Paul Eline. Engelhardt said to Eline:

> "Paul, I do not feel well. Please understand that I am an
> innocent man, who was wrongly convicted."[1]

Pennsylvania prison officials had already denied the
dying cleric critical medical care, and the next day, Fr.
Engelhardt died.

The coroner will tell you the cause of Fr. Engelhardt's
death was blocked arteries, but in truth, it was something far
more sinister that killed the priest.

Less than four year earlier, in January 2011, it was a story
that led televised newscasts and garnered front-page headlines
around the globe. A grand jury in Philadelphia convened by
District Attorney Seth Williams recommended that law

enforcement prosecute Fr. Engelhardt for rape of a child and other sex crimes. News of the grand jury report became a major worldwide story. For weeks, the news of "Catholic sex abuse in Philadelphia" was every bit as big as the story that broke in Boston nine years earlier in 2002.

And two years after the grand jury's recommendation, in January 2013, a criminal jury convicted Engelhardt of multiple sex crimes, including "indecent assault of a person under age 13." When Engelhardt died, he had not even served two years of his 6-to-12-year sentence.

But as is often the case with sensationalized news stories, the details surrounding the accusations against Engelhardt were lost. The media never revealed that the facts of Engelhardt's case showed that this was a priest that was clearly falsely accused.

The entire 2011 grand jury report largely centered around the eye-popping claims of a single individual whom the report only identified as "Billy." "Billy" was in fact a young man named Daniel Gallagher. Born in 1988 and raised in Northeast Philadelphia, Gallagher was only 20 years old when he told archdiocesan officials in February 2009 his stories of brutal sexual abuse by Engelhardt a decade earlier while serving as a 10-year-old altar boy at St. Jerome's Church.

But Gallagher did not only accuse Engelhardt of abuse. Gallagher also claimed that another priest (Fr. Edward Avery) and a school teacher (Bernard Shero) had abused him as well. In the end, Gallagher's tale was that a total of *three* men – two priests and a school teacher, all of whom barely knew each other – savagely assaulted him. They were stunning charges.

However, a number of troubling facts eventually emerged that cast major doubt upon Gallagher's credibility. They were facts that the media largely ignored:

- By his early twenties, Gallagher had already been arrested at least six times – once for possession of 56 bags of heroin – and had been in-and-out of some 23 drug rehabs.

- Gallagher had told drug counselors that he had been sexually abused at least six times as a young child by other individuals, including a friend, a neighbor, and a nameless "14-year-old boy." Ultimately, at a deposition in the spring of 2014, Gallagher admitted that none of that abuse ever happened, saying that he was "high on drugs" when he told his phony tales.[2]

- On three separate occasions, Gallagher told drug counselors that his older brother had been arrested for molestation. In truth, Gallagher's older brother, James Gallagher, was a recently licensed attorney in Pennsylvania and had never been arrested at all.

- Gallagher admitted that he lied when he said he worked as a paramedic and as a "professional surfer" (yes, a professional surfer from Northeast Philadelphia).

- Gallagher was refuted when he claimed that he was abused while in fifth grade and part of the church's bell choir maintenance crew, as only eighth graders were part of such a group.

Indeed, these facts alone would not have completely exonerated Fr. Engelhardt. But then even more troubling facts emerged.

When Dan Gallagher first approached archdiocesan officials to claim abuse by Engelhardt and the others, Gallagher claimed that Engelhardt had anally raped him in a sacristy after a Mass in a brutal episode that lasted four to five *hours.*[3]

But then in subsequent retellings of his claims, Gallagher completely changed his story. The four-to-five-hour episode of anal rape soon became an incident of oral sex. And even later the story of oral sex turned into a tale of mutual masturbation.[4]

In other words, in accusing three different men of sexually assaulting him, Gallagher was unable to keep all of his stories straight.

Gallagher also claimed that his hours-long attack occurred at an early 6:15am Mass before school. This claim was problematic for two reasons: Detailed altar schedules from the year of the alleged attack show that Gallagher never even served at a 6:15am Mass (nor at 6:30am, the real time of the Mass). In addition, Gallagher's tale of an hours-long anal rape would be tough to explain considering there was soon another early morning Mass afterwards at 8am.

For his part, Fr. Engelhardt easily passed a polygraph test denying that he abused Danny Gallagher or anyone, and the test administrator was a guy often hired by the Philadelphia District Attorney's Office. Fr. Engelhardt also waved his fifth amendment rights and voluntarily appeared before the Philadelphia grand jury in 2010. Engelhardt asserted his innocence and testified:

> "I have no knowledge of who the person is. If he's sitting in this room today, I can't pick him out ... I found it to be a very humbling thing to be called on the phone ... when you know, there was no truth or that was something unrealistic that was happening to you."[5]

Gallagher's claims against the other two individuals he accused of abuse were also problematic. Records revealed that Gallagher never even served as an altar boy at Mass with Rev. Avery, as Gallagher had claimed. And Gallagher's bizarre claims that school teacher Shero, who wore thick, Coke-bottle glasses and was legally blind, tied up Gallagher in the back seat of his car and sexually assaulted him required one to suspend all common sense. But, then again, Gallagher, who likely saw that his original story about Shero was a stretch, soon changed his tale into something else entirely.

Gallagher told tales of perverted abuse by a trio of men that not only varied wildly over time but also defied belief. And in a 2014 deposition, when attorneys questioned Gallagher about all the discrepancies in his stories, Gallagher responded by saying he couldn't remember *more than 130 times.*[6]

Fr. Engelhardt's religious order, The Oblates of St. Francis de Sales, continued to fight to clear Engelhardt's name even after the priest's death. And in October 2015, the order successfully forced Gallagher to be examined by a forensic psychiatrist. In a 40-page report, Dr. Stephen Mechanick concluded that Gallagher was indeed a troubled individual, but there was no evidence that he had ever been sexually abused. Mechanick described Gallagher in colorful terms throughout his report, writing, "The client is apparently immature and self-indulgent, manipulating others to his own ends ... chronically maladjusted ... He refuses to accept responsibility for his own problems ... hedonistic ... manipulative and self-serving ... He tends to blame others for problems he has helped to create ... delusional."[7]

Mechanick also suggested "the possibility that Mr. Gallagher reported that he was abused so that his parents and others might be less critical of him, and so that they might see him as a victim rather than being responsible for his drug abuse."[8]

But the greatest revelations of all about the fraudulence of Gallagher's accusations did not emerge until years after Engelhardt's trial and death.

Joseph Walsh was the lead detective in Fr. Engelhardt's case for the Philadelphia District Attorney's office when it originally examined Gallagher's claims in 2010. And in January 2017, Walsh filed a stunning, 12-page affidavit in Philadelphia Common Pleas Court. The detective wrote that he confronted Gallagher about the numerous inconsistencies, errors, and contradictions in his stories:

> "I asked [Gallagher], what he told [archdiocesan investigators and a drug counselor], all those graphic details did he just make all that up? **He said he just made up stuff and told them anything.** So I asked him, did he lie about what happened … about what he said occurred. **He said yea I guess so. I asked him if he was lying about anything else and he would not answer me.** He just sat there and did not answer me."[9]

"I concluded Gallagher was not sexually abused by Fr. Engelhardt," Walsh wrote. (Walsh also concluded the same with regards to Gallagher's other two targets, Fr. Edward Avery and teacher Bernard Shero.)

There it was, in black and white. Daniel Gallagher *admitted* that he "just made stuff up."

All in all, members of the Philadelphia DA's office *knew full well* that Daniel Gallagher was not telling the truth, yet they still went forward with their prosecutions anyways. Walsh wrote that when he submitted his reports about

Gallagher's numerous problems to Assistant DA Mariana Sorensen, the main prosecutor of the cases, Sorensen shot back to Walsh, "You're killing my case"[10]

So *why* did the Philadelphia DA's office insist on moving forward with a prosecution that was so obviously phony? Well, it turns out that the 2011 grand jury report that felled Fr. Engelhardt and others was the *third* such report against the Catholic Church that the DA's office had written in less than a decade. (The first two (2003 and 2005) were under DA Lynne Abraham, and the 2011 report was completed under DA Seth Williams.[11] The first two reports did not yield any criminal charges.)

A Moby Dick-like obsession to target the Catholic Church permeated the Philadelphia DA's office, as evidenced by troubling alliances between members of the DA's office and the leadership of the lawyer-funded advocacy group SNAP (Survivors Network of those Abused by Priests). (See more on SNAP in Chapter 14.)

The efforts against the Church were largely driven by Assistant DA Mariana Sorensen, the primary author of both the 2005 and 2011 grand jury reports and an individual with a clear and profound animus against the Catholic Church. In 2006, Sorensen co-wrote a particularly nasty letter to then-Cardinal Justin Rigali of the Archdiocese of Philadelphia, recklessly accusing the archbishop of being callous and uncaring in light of priests committing "countless child rapes."[12] Also in 2006, Sorensen penned an opinion article for the *Philadelphia Inquirer* arguing for lifting the statute of limitations for abuse claims. Yet her desire for this legislation seemed almost singly rooted in her eagerness to punish the Catholic Church.[13]

Sorensen's 2005 grand jury report was so erroneous and hostile that the Archdiocese of Philadelphia actually issued a 73-page response to it. The archdiocese cited the report's "sensationalized, lurid, and tabloid-like presentation of events." It retorted that the report's reckless claims of a Church "cover-up" were "categorically false."[14]

And, indeed, Sorensen's 2005 report did not result in any criminal charges against the Archdiocese of Philadelphia. But Sorensen was clearly driven to change that with her next effort. When she came across Daniel Gallagher's lurid accusations, which still fell within the statute of limitations, Sorensen saw for herself a golden opportunity to finally put some Catholic clerics behind bars.

As for Gallagher, he just wanted to "get paid." In February 2009, nearly a full year before he met with the Philadelphia DA's office, Gallagher told a social worker for the Archdiocese of Philadelphia that "He has been talking to lawyers," and if "he gets money," he "does not want to press charges."[15]

Such a statement was surely the kind of evidence that a defense attorney would have wanted to show to a jury to prove that Gallagher was not really seeking justice for any abuse that he suffered but that he just wanted money. But even though the Philadelphia DA's office was in possession of these important notes taken by the archdiocesan social worker, it never turned them over (seven pages worth) to defense attorneys, as required by law. The notes did not surface until October of 2018, eight years after the DA's office first got a hold of them.[16]

But by 2018, the damage had already been long done, and, most notably, Gallagher had already achieved his goal to "get paid." In August 2015, Gallagher quietly scored a reported $5 million in a settlement with the Archdiocese of Philadelphia. He then continued to build a comfortable new life in sunny Florida.[17]

(How does an admitted liar and fraudster score a cool $5 million? Keep reading.)

Four innocent men (l to r): Fr. Charles Engelhardt, teacher Bernard Shero, Fr. Edward Avery, and Msgr. William J. Lynn all went to prison because of the incredible claims of criminal Daniel Gallagher, who admitted to a detective that he "just made stuff up."

Daniel Gallagher sent four innocent men to prison, scored $5 million from the Archdiocese of Philadelphia, and is now living in Florida.

NOTES

[1] Ralph Cipriano, "A Priest's Dying Declaration In Prison," BigTrial.net, December 31, 2014.
[2] Ralph Cipriano, "How To Collect $5 Million From The Archdiocese Of Philadelphia," BigTrial.net, March 18, 2016.
https://www.bigtrial.net/2016/03/how-to-collect-5-million-from.html
[3] Ralph Cipriano, "Judge Ceisler Puts Away Engelhardt And Shero," BigTrial.net, June 12, 2013.
[4] Ibid.
[5] Ralph Cipriano, "A Priest's Ordeal," BigTrial.net, June 4, 2013.
[6] Ralph Cipriano, "How To Collect $5 Million From The Archdiocese Of Philadelphia," BigTrial.net, March 18, 2016.
[7] Ralph Cipriano, "Newsweek's Cover Boy Makes A Splash," BigTrial.net, January 28, 2016.
[8] Ibid.
[9] "Information from Retired Detective Joseph Walsh #697," affidavit filed in January 2017.
[10] "Information from Retired Detective Joseph Walsh #697," affidavit filed in January 2017.
[11] Unrelated to the Church abuse cases, in March 2017, Philadelphia DA Seth Williams was indicted on 23 counts of bribery and corruption. According to a federal indictment (Eastern District of Pennsylvania), Williams "solicited, accepted, and agreed to accept" gifts including round-trip trips to the Dominican Republic, Las Vegas, California, and Florida; Luis Vuitton clothing; a Jaguar XK8 convertible; thousands in cash, and more. And if this were not enough, Williams also stole money from his own adoptive mother.
[12] The text of Sorensen's letter is available at TheMediaReport.com:
http://www.themediareport.com/wp-content/uploads/2012/04/Sorensen-McCartney-072606-letter-Card-Rigali.pdf
[13] Mariana C. Sorensen, "One year on, no fix in abuse laws," *The Philadelphia Inquirer*, September 28, 2006.
[14] Stradley, Ronon, Stevens & Young LLP, Attorneys for The

Archdiocese of Philadelphia, "Response of the Archdiocese of Philadelphia to the Report of the Investigating Grand Jury Pursuant to PA. C.S. § 4552(e)," 2005.

[15] Ralph Cipriano, "Old Notes Show That 'Billy Doe' Only Wanted $$$, But D.A. Hid Evidence," BigTrial.net, October 25, 2018.

[16] Ibid.

[17] Ralph Cipriano, "How To Collect $5 Million From The Archdiocese Of Philadelphia," BigTrial.net, March 18, 2016.

2

A Lesson From Pope Francis

One of the most astonishing false accusations in the entire Catholic Church abuse narrative involves Pope Francis.

In late 2014, as reported in a front-page story in the *New York Times*, Pope Francis responded to an emotional five-page letter he had just received and personally telephoned a 25-year-old man from Spain going by the name of "Daniel." Daniel – whose real name turned out to be David Ramírez Castillo – had written to the pope claiming that he and others had been repeatedly sexually abused years earlier as children by a ring of pedophile priests.

"I have read your letter several times," Francis reportedly told Castillo. "I could not help feeling terribly pained in reading your story. I want to apologize to you on behalf of the entire Church of Christ. Forgive this grave sin and the very serious crime that you have suffered."[1]

"The truth is the truth and we should not hide it," the pope added.[2] So emotionally moved by his letter, Pope Francis reportedly invited Castillo to be a member of the Vatican's prestigious Pontifical Commission for the Protection of Minors that advises the pope.[3]

Here were some of the news headlines at the time:

"Letter to Pope uncovers pedophile network in Spain" (Cruxnow.com, Nov. 18, 2014);
"Ten Catholic priests are charged with sexually abusing four altar boys in Spain after one of the alleged victims wrote to the Pope" (*Daily Mail*, Jan. 28, 2015);
"'I Am Father Jorge': Pope Phones A Sex-Abuse Victim and Causes a Stir in Spain" (Aleteia, Nov 20, 2014);
"In Spanish Abuse Scandal, a More Open Vatican," (*New York Times*, Feb. 15, 2015).

The *New York Times* reported that Castillo claimed that starting at age 14 in 2004, a priest repeatedly abused him and forced him to watch the priest and other priests have sex. The accusations were even "supported by one other plaintiff as well as by several witnesses," according to the *Times*. The paper then soberly informed its readers that the case was "one of the most serious sexual abuse scandals to emerge under Pope Francis."[4]

Acting upon Francis' urging, Spanish law enforcement promptly launched a criminal investigation. Police soon claimed that it had "uncovered a criminal network of pedophiles that involves at least 12 people among priests and laity from different parishes in the Spanish city of Granada."[5] Ten priests were indicted for either abusing Castillo or "covering up" the priests' alleged crimes.[6]

But then came the truth. Castillo's entire story turned out to be completely bogus. None of the abuse that attracted the Pope's personal attention and international headlines was true. None of it. It was all a crock.

In April 2017, almost two-and-a-half years after the original accusations – and after months of the media telling tales of rape, orgies, and pornography by priests – a Spanish court issued an exhaustive 81-page ruling exonerating *all* of the accused clerics. The report explained that Castillo's accusations were not just false for a lack of evidence, but they also were "completely implausible" as well as "contradictory, hesitant and uncorroborated."[7] The court's report also listed several events and details from the accuser that were proven to be outright false. The report underscored that there was "no evidence whatsoever" to support Castillo's accusations.[8]

For a reason God only knows, the accuser made the whole story up.

Remember: the *New York Times* had published the claim that there were "several witnesses" to the abuse. But there were zero. None. It was complete bunk. The reputations of numerous Spanish priests were forever shattered.

And whereas the original accusations against the priests garnered headlines and breathless news coverage around the world, when the truth emerged years later, the media coverage hardly reached the level of a whisper.

NOTES

[1] Jesús Bastante, "Francisco fuerza una investigación sobre abusos sexuales en una diócesis Española," *Periodista Digital*, November 16,

2014, Translated from Spanish from
https://www.periodistadigital.com/cultura/religion/espana/20141116
/francisco-fuerza-investigacion-abusos-sexuales-diocesis-espanola-
noticia-689401915463/, April 2020

[2] Raphael Minder, "In Spanish Abuse Scandal, a More Open Vatican,"
The New York Times, February 15, 2015, p. A1.

[3] Castillo reportedly declined the invitation to join the commission.
Michael Cook, "Let's all take a chill pill," Mercator.net, September 3,
2018. https://mercatornet.com/lets-all-take-a-chill-pill/23541/,
accessed in April 2020.

[4] Minder.

[5] Inés San Martín, "Letter to Pope uncovers pedophile network in
Spain," Cruxnow.com, November 18, 2014,
https://cruxnow.com/church/2014/11/letter-to-pope-uncovers-
pedophile-network-in-spain/

[6] Minder.

[7] "Father Román Martínez, acquitted of the crime of sexual abuse,"
InfoCatólica, April 11, 2017. English translation from Spanish,
http://www.infocatolica.com/?t=noticia&cod=29075 , April 2020.

[8] Ibid.

3

The Luck of the Irish

Why did Pope Francis simply assume that the abuse claims in the letter written to him were true? Well, the entire episode epitomizes how that even from regular parishioners in the pews to the highest levels of the Catholic hierarchy, the *mere accusation* against a Catholic priest carries an automatic assumption that the claim is true.

This is the very root of the problem of the media's coverage of the Catholic Church sex abuse story for the past 35 years. Indeed, as a lawyer opined years ago, Catholic priests are "guilty until proven guiltier."[1]

A dangerous groupthink has enveloped the media's reporting of the Catholic Church abuse scandals. And there was a particular episode in Ireland in 2011 that underscores the damage that unfettered groupthink can inflict.

In May of 2011, RTÉ, the national media outlet of Ireland, aired a primetime television special called *Mission to Prey*, which purported to chronicle cases of Irish priests who abused children decades earlier while working as missionaries overseas.

The program profiled the case of Fr. Kevin Reynolds and charged that Reynolds had both brutally raped and impregnated a young girl decades earlier in Kenya. Fr. Reynolds had also abandoned his child, the show claimed.[2]

Two weeks before the program aired, RTÉ reporter Aoife Kavanagh ambushed Fr. Reynolds as he exited his vehicle at his residence after having just presided at an annual First Communion Mass. Her opening salvo to the priest: "Thirty years ago, Father … You had a daughter who was born in Kenya."[3]

Fr. Reynolds vehemently denied he had ever committed anything like what was alleged. And in the days and weeks leading up to the program, Reynolds' attorneys repeatedly pressed the station not to air the accusations against Reynolds and even offered that Reynolds take a paternity test to prove the claims against him were false.

But RTÉ would have none of Reynolds' pestering proclamations of innocence. The network even claimed that it had a "very credible third-party source" to support its claims against Reynolds. RTÉ then aired its program.

Yet a paternity test soon proved that Fr. Reynolds was entirely innocent. He was not the father of any child. There was no rape. And there certainly was not any "very credible third-party source," as the producers at the network had claimed. When Fr. Reynolds loudly proclaimed his innocence, he was being entirely truthful.

In the end, RTÉ was not only forced to apologize to Reynolds, but it also paid a costly 200,000 Euro fine to the Broadcasting Authority of Ireland (BAI) as well as a sizable settlement to Reynolds himself. The *Irish Times* reported the settlement to Reynolds as "more than €1 million, including costs."[4] It was a watershed moment.

In the wake of the defamation of Fr. Reynolds and the complete abandonment of journalistic standards at RTÉ, the BAI commissioned a report to investigate how such a disaster could have unfolded at the network. To no one's surprise, the report concluded, "There was a significant failure of RTÉ's editorial and managerial controls in advance of the broadcast. This in turn led to a failure to anticipate or recognize the potential for grave injustice against Fr Reynolds and the reputational damage which could be done to RTÉ's journalism."[5]

In other words, the consideration that Fr. Reynolds was telling the truth when he denied the accusations against him was not even on the radar at RTÉ.

The report also added that a **"groupthink mentality"** had enveloped the production team to the point where "they were convinced that the facts verified their assumption."[6] And rather than believing that Fr. Reynolds' offer to take a paternity test was a genuine attempt to establish his innocence, producers at RTÉ held the collective belief that it was merely at "tactic" by Reynolds "to derail the program."[7]

The entire episode also raised an important question, but one which very few bothered to ask following RTÉ's debacle: *What if the allegation against Fr. Reynolds was of a type that could not have been disproved by a paternity test?* Columnist David Quinn of the *Irish Independent* was a singular voice who asked:

"Supposed [RTÉ] had said merely that [Fr. Reynolds] had raped someone. That can't be scientifically falsified. What *can* be scientifically falsified is the claim that he fathered a child. So if no claim had been made that he had fathered a child, would any investigation into *Mission to Prey* whatsoever have taken place?"[8]

The clear answer to Quinn's question is an obvious "no." There is no doubt that if Fr. Reynolds was not "lucky" enough to have been accused of fathering a child and thus able to *prove* his innocence, he would be long out of ministry and forever remembered as a just another "child molesting predator priest."

Accused Catholic priests frequently assert their innocence, but the default response to their claims is to simply assume without any thought that they are lying. It is a common practice among the media – and everyone – and it needs to stop.

Essential questions: How does one defend oneself against an accusation from 30, 40, 50 years ago? How would *you* defend yourself against an accusation from 40 years ago?

Here is RTÉ reporter Aoife Kavanagh ambushing Fr. Kevin Reynolds in May 2011 after a First Communion Mass and accusing the priest, "Thirty years ago, Father ... You had a daughter who was born in Kenya." It was all false.

NOTES

[1] Telephone interview with Joseph Maher in Summer 2010. Maher now operates Men of Melchizedek, an organization dedicated to facilitating help for priests who are in need. Men of Melchizedek is at https://menofmelchizedek.org/

[2] "Fr Kevin Reynolds, RTÉ defamation case settled," RTÉ, Friday, 18 November 2011, https://www.rte.ie/news/2011/1117/308846-reynoldsk/

[3] Louise Hogan, "Absence of 'evidence, scrutiny and challenge' in high-risk programme," *Irish Independent*, May 5, 2012.

[4] "RTÉ to pay damages to priest over abuse libel," Irish Times, Friday, 18 November 2011, https://www.irishtimes.com/news/rt%C3%A9-to-pay-damages-to-priest-over-abuse-libel-1.13018

[5] "Report cites a groupthink atmosphere of unchallenged assumptions," *Irish Times*, Tue, Apr 10, 2012. https://www.irishtimes.com/news/report-cites-a-groupthink-atmosphere-of-unchallenged-assumptions-1.498232

[6] Ibid.

[7] Ibid.

[8] "Prime Time: Standards Investigated," quote from David Quinn of the *Irish Independent*, https://www.youtube.com/watch?v=urBD2NRKwSo , Wed.., April 11, 2012.

4

The Truth About
False Accusations

In commenting on the wave of lawsuits against the
Catholic Church over claims of abuse from decades earlier,
Wall Street Journal writer Dorothy Rabinowitz once remarked:

> "People have to come to understand that there is a large scam
> going on with personal injury attorneys, and what began as a
> serious effort has now expanded to become a huge money-
> making proposition."[1]

And Ms. Rabinowitz made her statement back in 2005.

Some people bristle at merely bringing up the issue of
false accusations, thinking that it is somehow an insult to
victims whose dignities were so violated by criminal priests.
In truth, however, a false accusation is a gross offense to
bonafide victims. Whether it be made for financial gain,
public attention, or the result of mental illness,[2] a false
accusation is truly an affront to those who genuinely suffered
as the result of their horrendous abuse.

With that said, it must be stressed that bogus abuse accusations against Catholic priests are rampant. The fraud being perpetrated against the Catholic Church is a harsh reality. While there is not yet a singular widespread study that has tabulated the prevalence of false accusations, there are a number of sources that indicate their pervasiveness.

- In 2011, lawyer Donald H. Steier submitted a declaration to the Los Angeles County Superior Court asserting that a former FBI investigator examining abuse claims against priests in Los Angeles had determined that "ONE-HALF of the claims were either entirely false or so greatly exaggerated that the truth would not have supported a prosecutable claim for childhood sexual abuse." (The capital letters are in the original document.)

Mr. Steier also added, "In several cases my investigation has provided objective information that could not be reconciled with the truthfulness of the subjective allegations. In other words, in many cases objective facts showed that accusations were false … [S]everal plaintiffs testified that they realized that they had been abused only after learning that some other person – sometimes a relative – had received a financial settlement from the Archdiocese or another Catholic institution."[3]

- According to a recent annual report examining abuse in the Catholic Church, in a church of 70 million people in the United States, 25 minors came forward alleging that a current priest had recently abused them. Some of the cases still remained under investigation when the report was being released, but of the 13 allegations in which a determination was made, only *two* were found to be "substantiated," while the remaining 11 (or *85%*) were found to be false.[4]

That same report also found that only 15% of *all* accusations against Catholic priests – including those against dead priests going back decades – were deemed "substantiated" by the very lenient standards of diocesan review boards, with the majority of accusations deemed either "unsubstantiated" (indeed *false* (see next page)), "unable to be proven," or still under review.[5]

● The Archdiocese of Boston has arguably been the most transparent when it comes to releasing names of its accused priests. It publishes the names of all publicly accused priests on its web site and often updates its lists. Boston has published the names of 58 priests who have been determined guilty of abuse by either canonical or civil proceedings. Yet the diocese's lists also show that 37 priests have been falsely accused. In other words, more than one in three accused priests in Boston (38.9%) are determined innocent after a complete investigation.[6] (*NB*: In recent years, unsubstantiated allegations have far outnumbered substantiated ones. Since 2012, 13 names have been added to the "unsubstantiated" list, while only five have been added to the "substantiated.")

Predictably, these sobering facts have been almost completely absent in the media's reporting.

Again, the *vast majority* of claims from the individuals who first came forward decades ago were true. Today, however, the pendulum has swung completely in the other direction, and it is the assessment of this author that *at least* 85% of claims being filed today are fraudulent.

FAST FACT: There has been confusion about what is meant by an "unsubstantiated" allegation. When a diocese determines an accusation to be "unsubstantiated," it adheres to the definition as defined by annual reports conducted by independent auditors: "'Unsubstantiated' describes an allegation for which an investigation is complete and the allegation has been **deemed not credible/false based upon the evidence gathered through the investigation**."

Indeed, "unsubstantiated" allegations are those that have been fully investigated and determined to be *false*.

The last true journalist?

Honest journalism: Philadelphia's Ralph Cipriano

Chapter 1 of this book chronicled how the claims of a criminal fraudster in Philadelphia sent three innocent clerics and a teacher to prison. And it must be noted that this injustice never would have seen the light of day except for one intrepid journalist.

In 2012, when Ralph Cipriano began covering the Philadelphia clergy abuse cases, he admitted he approached the cases as "pro-prosecution," meaning, like almost all people, he assumed the clerics were guilty as the Philadelphia DA's office and the media reported. Cipriano already had a well-established track record of criticizing the Archdiocese of Philadelphia, so Cipriano was no ally of the Catholic Church.

When accuser Daniel Gallagher delivered in court his testimony of incredible stories of rape and assault by Catholic priests, the *Philadelphia Inquirer*, the Associated Press, and other news outlets simply relayed Gallagher's claims as if they were unquestionably true. But Cipriano grew suspicious. Gallagher's claims were just too ridiculous to believe.

Cipriano investigated Gallagher's criminal background and examined his claims. Nearly *everything* we came to learn about the egregious prosecutorial malpractice in Philadelphia came from Cipriano. He has reported everything he has discovered on the site BigTrial.net.

Imagine if every city had a Ralph Cipriano, a journalist who critically examines facts and not just parrots the press releases of prosecutors and contingency lawyers. It would provide perspective, truth, and justice that are so sorely needed in today's media landscape.

NOTES

[1] Daniel Barrick, "Writer takes up convicted priest's case," *Concord Monitor*, April 29, 2005.

---

[2] This author's second book, published in 2012, *Catholic Priests Falsely Accused*, explored some of the major reasons why false accusations are made against priests.

[3] TheMediaReport.com, "Los Angeles Attorney Declares Rampant Fraud, Many Abuse Claims Against Catholic Priests are 'Entirely False'," January 2, 2011.

[4] United States Conference of Catholic Bishops, "2016 Annual Report: Findings and Recommendations," May 2017.

[5] Ibid.

[6] The list of accused priests can be found at https://www.bostoncatholic.org/offices-and-services/accused-clergy ... The list of unsubstantiated cases is at https://www.bostoncatholic.org/protecting-children-word-welcome/list-unsubstantiated-cases

5

A Grand Fraud in Pennsylvania

No other episode in the Catholic Church sex abuse story has epitomized the reality of "groupthink mentality" than the composition, release, and aftermath of the Pennsylvania grand jury report from the summer of 2018.

On August 14, 2018, Pennsylvania Attorney General Josh Shapiro stood in front of an enormous throng of national and international media to make the incredible claim that a grand jury had determined that "over 300 priests" in Pennsylvania had sexually abused "over 1,000 victims" in the last several decades.

And if that were not shocking enough, Shapiro boldly asserted to the world that Church officials "did nothing" about the abuse and "they covered it all up."

Every action by Shapiro was a masterful stroke of public relations to maximize media exposure and enhance his own public profile. Shapiro carefully orchestrated a news conference with Hollywood-type preparation. Whereas a typical news conference would contain a simple setup with a podium and a few associates standing beside him, Shapiro took everything to a whole new level.

Shapiro called a local poster company to create a new, official-looking seal to be placed behind him as he broadcast his "grand jury report" to the world. Whereas the official seal of his office normally displayed the words "Commonwealth of Pennsylvania" along the top and "Office of the Attorney General" along the bottom, Shapiro not only flipped them around, but he also completely replaced the words "Office of the Attorney General" with "Attorney General Josh Shapiro" so everyone across the globe could now easily see his name behind his head as he stood at the podium.[1]

On the left is the official seal for the Pennsylvania Attorney General. But Josh Shapiro had a special one made just for his press conference so everyone would be sure to see his name behind his head.

Shapiro's entire event, from the lighting to the staging, rivaled a primetime network entertainment show.

But Shapiro's Hollywood-style press conference notwithstanding, the central question remained: Were the claims from Shapiro's grand jury report actually *true*? Did "over 300 priests" really abuse "over 1,000 victims" while Church officials "did nothing"?

In a nutshell, no. Not at all.

First of all, it is essential to know what a "grand jury report" actually is. As any lawyer will tell you, a "grand jury report" is simply a report written by government attorneys with a predetermined outcome. The folks in the "jury," although they dedicate a lot of time, are merely a formality, window dressing to make the entire matter legal. The jurors do not actually investigate a case, question witnesses, scrutinize all sides of a story, and then sit down together at a computer and carefully compose a 1,100-page report.

Rather, jurors sit in a room eating hoagies and reading the newspaper while "listening" to one-sided proceedings orchestrated by prosecutors.[2] There is no fact-checking, no cross-examination of witnesses, and no due process.

A large team of taxpayer-funded government attorneys create the message that it wants the public to hear, and when the time comes, a jury member simply slaps his signature on the finished product to make everything official.

Properly used, a grand jury is merely supposed to examine evidence to determine whether there is probable cause that a crime took place and if it should be prosecuted. This was clearly not the intention of Josh Shapiro. One can see this in nearly every page of his 1100-page report.

For starters, Shapiro's report treated each and every accusation as if they were true, no matter what the findings of civil and Church investigators were. And, needless to say, media outlets around the globe seized upon the most sensational accusations in Shapiro's report.

One such case was that involving Msgr. Thomas Benestad, who served in the Diocese of Allentown with a completely unblemished record until 2007, when he retired from full-time ministry for health reasons.

In 2011, a man e-mailed the Diocese of Allentown claiming that he had a "memory" from thirty years earlier that, starting at nine years old, he was regularly pulled out of Sunday school class on a weekly basis for oral sex for over two years. The accuser said a nun would escort him to Benestad's office where Benestad would force him to perform oral sex on him.

But that's not all. After he was finished, the accuser claimed, Benestad would perform oral sex on him as well. And then Benestad would magically "produce a clear bottle of holy water and squirt it into the victim's mouth to purify him." (Because what priest doesn't keep a "clear bottle of holy water" handy at all times?)

Shapiro's report excoriated the Diocese of Allentown for having "elected to rely on Benestad's word rather than the word of the victim." What the report completely failed to mention, however, was that Benestad's case had been thoroughly examined by a former FBI agent who determined the claim to be completely bogus. Shapiro also neglected to note that the accuser was a serial criminal with incarcerations in multiple states and had been diagnosed with serious mental illness.[3] And if Shapiro's office had made the effort to speak to the nun who allegedly "escorted" the boy to Benestad's office on a weekly basis, the nun would have said that no such thing ever occurred and would have questioned Msgr. Benestad if something like that had.

Yet in the days and weeks following the release of the grand jury report, countless writers would cite Benestad's case as the one in which a priest "forced a boy to wash his mouth out with holy water after oral sex." Not only did almost all major media outlets not tell their audiences that Benestad vehemently denied the charges against him, but they also did not report that the claims were thoroughly investigated and found to be false.

Several media outlets also trumpeted the alarming claims in the report from a man named "George," who says he was the victim of multiple episodes of abuse involving whips, violence, and sadism, by not one, not two, but *four* different priests. On one occasion, George said he was forced onto a bed, ordered to take off his clothes, and pose like Jesus on the cross. He then claimed the priests "began taking Polaroid pictures" of him which were later "added to a collection of similar photographs depicting other teenage boys."

George also went on to claim that for his actions he was given a gold cross for being one of the priests' "favorite boys."[4]

The depravity of the allegations is chilling, indeed. But the report completely failed to mention that "George" had never even come forward to the Diocese of Pittsburgh or law enforcement before. His identity and personal history are still a complete mystery. Despite George's claim that the crimes occurred around 1980, he never came forward in the late 1980s, 1992, 2002, 2010, or any of the other previous years that Catholic sex abuse had made worldwide headlines.

And it turns out that three of the priests that he accused had already been criminally convicted and/or removed from active priesthood in the late 1980s. News outlets had already chronicled their cases, and the stories were widely available to read about on the Internet. In a news account from November 1988 in which criminal charges against the trio were announced, a prosecutor said that "some of the incidents involved whips, chains, drugs and alcohol,"[5] which is startling similar to what George claimed.

And while George claimed that the four priests criminally exploited him within the same rectory, a thorough investigation back in the 1980s determined that the priests never acted together. An examination of personnel files shows that the four priests were ordained many years apart from each other and worked in four totally different parishes, some of them dozens of miles apart. Indeed, a case in which multiple priests from four separate churches sexually assaulted a single youth in the same room would be unprecedented in the entire Catholic Church sex abuse narrative.

George also claimed that Polaroid pictures taken of him posed as Jesus were placed into a "collection," yet no such photographs depicting George were ever uncovered. In addition, while the report says George befriended one of the priests in the "mid-1970s," records show that the priest was not even ordained until 1980.

In the end, the media uncritically trumpeted the claims from "George" as if they were established fact, yet there were plenty of reasons to question the veracity of his accusations.

Rinsing victims' mouths with holy water and making one boy pose as Jesus: Grand Jury reveals the depravity of 301 priests who sexually assaulted at least 1,000 children - which the Catholic church covered up

- The 900 page grand jury report is based on records from six dioceses
- It puts the 'real number' of child victims 'in the thousands'
- One group of priests is accused of producing child porn and using whips on children

News outlets across the world relayed the most frightful stories from Josh Shapiro's grand jury report as if they were undeniably true. In fact, they were not. (Image from the UK's DailyMail, August 2018.)

FAST FACTS: This author identified 233 accused individuals in the 2018 Pennsylvania report who were named and whose living status was noted. Of those 233 priests, 124 of them, or over 53%, were deceased, and thus no longer around to defend themselves. (The status of about 20 men in the report were listed as "unknown"; 20 entries were blacked out (redacted) completely; and there were about 13 others who were not even listed with a name (e.g., "Pittsburgh priests #2-10," "Harrisburg priest #1," etc.).)

One accused priest was born in **1869**, four years after the end of the Civil War, when the USA consisted of only 37 states, and a decade before Thomas Edison invented the light bulb.

NOTES

[1] Richard Lavinthal, "Shapiro's slickly managed press conference

stepped on his message," *Patriot News*,
https://www.pennlive.com/opinion/2018/08/shapiros_slickly_manage
d_press.html, Aug. 17, 2018.

[2] Ralph Cipriano, "A Priest's Ordeal," BigTrial.net, June 4, 2013,
http://www.bigtrial.net/2013/06/a-priests-ordeal.html

[3] "Reality Check: Five Fast Facts You Need to Know About the
Overhyped PA Grand Jury Report," TheMediaReport.com,
http://www.themediareport.com/2018/09/04/pennsylvania-jury-
report-fast-facts/, September 4, 2018.

[4] "Report of the 40th Statewide Investigating Grand Jury," July 27,
2018 (pdf online). Accessed April 2020
https://www.attorneygeneral.gov/wp-content/uploads/2018/08/A-
Report-of-the-Fortieth-Statewide-Investigating-Grand-Jury_Cleland-
Redactions-8-12-08_Redacted.pdf

[5] Associated Press, "Three Priests Charged with Sex Abuse,"
November 11, 1988. Accessed http://www.bishop-
accountability.org/news3/1988_11_11_AP_ThreePriests_Francis_Pucc
i_etc_2.htm

6

Pennsylvania Perjury

Probably the most explosive charge from Josh Shapiro's grand jury report was in its first few pages:

> "Priests were raping little boys and girls, and the men of God who were responsible for them not only did nothing. They hid it all."

Did Pennsylvania bishops really "do nothing" when confronted with news that priests had criminally harmed children? No. Even Shapiro's own report shows that his claim is false.

One bishop whom Shapiro targeted in his report was Bishop Donald Walter Trautman, who led the Diocese of Erie from 1990 until 2012. The report portrayed Trautman as if he had given child molesters free reign to run wild in his diocese.

Yet during his tenure, Bishop Trautman removed nearly two dozen clerics from ministry for sex crimes and petitioned most of them to be removed from the priesthood.

One such case involved Salvatore Luzzi. In 1994, when Trautman got word that Luzzi had groped juveniles, Trautman took him out of ministry and shipped him off to an inpatient therapy facility, which (as we will see in Chapter 8) was a common practice in the mid-1990s. Not satisfied with the aftermath of his treatment, Trautman completely removed Luzzi's faculties, and the man never worked as a priest again. Contrary to Shapiro's claim, Trautman did not "do nothing."

The report also went to great lengths to take issue with Trautman's handling of a priest named David Poulson, who was arrested in May of 2018 on the eve of Shapiro's report. But Shapiro failed to mention that there were never any complaints of misconduct against children by Poulson at any time during Trautman's tenure.

In 2010, Trautman *did* receive a "fourth-hand" allegation of misconduct with an adult male, but after numerous letters and phone calls by diocesan officials to try and talk to the guy, there was never any response. Trautman had no choice but to keep Poulson in ministry.[1]

Eight years later, law enforcement arrested Poulson for the sexual abuse of two boys from years earlier, and the media claimed that Trautman had somehow "covered up" misconduct by Poulson. Trautman replied, "Why would I cover up Poulson's sinful behavior when I had removed 22 priests from ministry and sought their dismissal from the clerical state?"[2] It was a fair question. In a statement, Trautman also added:

"I devoted a significant part of my tenure as bishop of the Diocese of Erie to the important issue of abuse within the church ... I took the problem of sexual abuse seriously and was aggressive in the removal of abusive priests from the service of God's people. I wish to emphasize again that there was no cover-up."[3]

Another major target of Shapiro's report was Cardinal Donald W. Wuerl, who served as Bishop of the Diocese of Pittsburgh from 1988 to 2006. As with Bishop Trautman, what Shapiro published in his report was often far different than what actually transpired.

Even a cursory review of Wuerl's record in his handling of criminal sex abuse cases renders Shapiro's claim that Wuerl "did nothing" as absurd.

For example, in 1986, when a man approached the Diocese of Pittsburgh to claim that Rev. Joseph Mueller abused him years earlier as a teenager, diocesan officials immediately removed Mueller from ministry and shipped him off to an inpatient treatment facility. Based on its evaluation of the guy, doctors advised that Mueller "not work with children or adolescents," and Wuerl received a letter declaring that Mueller was "unassignable." So what did Wuerl do? He completely stripped Mueller of his faculties, and the man never worked as a priest ever again.

An examination of the record shows that Cardinal Wuerl was very aggressive with the issue of clergy sex abuse. Within mere months of taking office in Pittsburgh in 1988, Bishop Wuerl made the matter an important focus of his episcopate and soon created a Diocesan Review Board – which may have been the first of its kind in the country – to review abuse cases brought before it.

Composed primarily of lay experts on sex abuse, social workers, and law enforcement personnel, the board had "extreme independence," according to Fred Thieman, a former U.S. attorney and longtime chairman of the board. "We were given the freedom to reach whatever decisions we wanted to reach, based on the best evidence," said Thieman. And Bishop Wuerl made decisions on priests only after hearing the board's evaluation and recommendations.[4]

One particular case that was emblematic of Wuerl's toughness toward abusive priests was a case from the late 1980s and early 1990s involving Fr. Anthony J. Cipolla. After accusations that Cipolla had abused teenage boys, Bishop Wuerl revoked the faculties of Cipolla such that he could never work as a priest again. But Cipolla appealed his case to the Vatican, and in 1993, the Vatican ordered that Wuerl reinstate Cipolla as a priest in good standing.

Remarkably, Wuerl refused the Vatican's request and petitioned the Vatican court to hear Cipolla's case again. Wuerl even travelled to Rome to argue his position. Two years later, the Vatican reversed its previous decision, keeping Cipolla out of ministry. Wuerl prevailed.

"That decision provided an example for fellow bishops to deal effectively with sexually abusive priest," Wuerl later wrote.[5]

In the ensuing years, Wuerl developed such a strong reputation for being tough on sex abuse that when Cardinal Bernard Law resigned as Archbishop of Boston in December 2002 there was speculation that Wuerl would be assigned there. The media at the time even quoted an abuse victim in the Diocese of Pittsburgh as saying, "If you're looking for a bishop who is going to oust these priests, he is the man for you."[6]

Wuerl's most impactful practice, however, may have been his insistence that he personally meet with victims and their families if they desired to do so. This was done over the loud objection of diocesan lawyers, whose primary concern was that such meetings could further expose the diocese to liability.

Wuerl's first such meeting was in 1988 with victims and their families who had only recently been victimized by criminal priests. "As their bishop I was responsible for the Church's care of that family, and the only way I could do that was to go see them," Wuerl said.

"You can't be part of a meeting like that without realizing the horrific pain and damage that abuse causes," added Bishop David Zubik, who, as a diocesan priest at the time, also attended the same meeting.[7]

Yet as the firestorm from Josh Shapiro's 2018 grand jury report spread, the media's portrayal of Wuerl and his track record on abuse soon became far detached from the truth.

Cardinal Wuerl understandably objected strongly to Shapiro's claim that he had shown "disdain for victims." "That's simply not verified with the facts … I met with every victim. Anyone that would come forward, I met with them and I'd have to say more than once shared a tear with them as they or their parents told the story," Cardinal Wuerl said after the release of Shapiro's report.[8]

The front page of the October 28, 1988, edition of the Diocese of Pittsburgh newspaper showed that combatting sex abuse by priests was a major priority for Bishop Wuerl.

NOTES

[1] "Statement from Bishop Emeritus Donald W. Trautman regarding David Poulson," May 9, 2018, retrieved from https://www.goerie.com/assets/PA3027959.PDF

[2] Matthew Rink, "Trautman denies cover-up in priest sex-abuse case," GoErie.com, May 15, 2018, https://www.goerie.com/news/20180515/trautman-denies-cover-up-in-priest-sex-abuse-case

[3] Statement from Bishop Emeritus Donald W. Trautman regarding David Poulson

[4] Ann Rodgers, "Zero tolerance for abuse: Pittsburgh Bishop Donald Wuerl's approach to abuse survivors was, 'I'm their bishop, and I need to respond to their pain'," *Catholic Standard*, November 22, 2016.

[5] "Response for the Catholic Diocese of Pittsburgh to Report of the 40th Statewide Investigating Grand Jury," July/August 2018.

[6] Ann Rodgers-Melnick, "Wuerl's tough record on sex abuse spurs speculation of move to Boston," *Pittsburgh Post-Gazette*, June 15, 2003.

7 Ann Rodgers, "Zero tolerance for abuse: Pittsburgh Bishop Donald Wuerl's approach to abuse survivors was, 'I'm their bishop, and I need to respond to their pain'," *Catholic Standard*, November 22, 2016.

8 Tom Fitzgerald, "Cardinal Wuerl addresses report on child sex abuse by priests, says he will not resign" Fox5DC (television interview, video), August 20, 2018, Accessed at https://www.fox5dc.com/news/cardinal-wuerl-addresses-report-on-child-sex-abuse-by-priests-says-he-will-not-resign

7

Nowhere To Be Found

The 2018 Pennsylvania grand jury report by Josh Shapiro also marked an important moment in the Catholic Church for another reason that most Catholics did not notice. It marked an astonishing moment when the Catholic media in the United States decided to go completely silent in defending bishops, priests, and the Church when they were publicly wronged.

Since the media's coverage of the Catholic Church sex abuse story began in 1985, the Catholic media would often provide a reliable counterpoint and perspective when unfair or inaccurate media coverage would emerge.

One such example is from 2010, when the *New York Times'* "National Religion Correspondent" Laurie Goodstein composed a series of articles about a decades-old case of a notorious priest from Milwaukee. The case received worldwide media attention for Goodstein's claims that the Vatican had showed "no thought at all about the victims" of the priest. But a number of Catholic media outlets provided powerful factual rebuttals to Goodstein's reporting and showed that key aspects of her reporting were outright erroneous.[1]

Indeed, when a media outlet would garner a lot of attention for an attack on the Catholic Church that was inaccurate or unfair, one could often look to writers in the Catholic media for a reliable reply.[2]

But in the summer of 2018, when Pennsylvania Attorney General Josh Shapiro released his breathless, 1,100-page report claiming that 300 priests had sexually abused "over 1,000" victims, almost the entire Catholic media landscape, including the Catholic blogosphere, was radio silent.

Like the apostles on the morning of Jesus' crucifixion, Catholic media voices were nowhere to be found.

Meanwhile, prominent writers with a dislike for the Catholic Church saw an opening to attack the Church, and these voices were soon publishing falsehoods and erroneous information. In a series of breathless posts in the aftermath of the Pennsylvania report, popular Methodist-turned-Catholic-turned-Orthodox blogger Rod Dreher wrote:

"[I]n 1991, Bishop Wuerl approved pedophile Pittsburgh priest Father [Ernest C.] Paone's assignment in the Diocese of Reno-Las Vegas. That priest continued to work there — without Pittsburgh telling them that they knew he was a pedophile — until the Boston scandal broke in 2002."[3]

It was a damning charge, indeed, but Dreher's claim was false. In truth, when Bishop Wuerl approved Paone's 1991 transfer, he was completely unaware of any accusations against him. It was not until 1994, three years later, when a woman approached the Diocese of Pittsburgh to claim that her brother had been molested by Paone some three decades earlier. Upon receiving this news, Wuerl immediately fired off a letter to the Diocese of Reno-Las Vegas. Wuerl wrote:

> "Very recently, an allegation was made by a woman who claims that more than 30 years ago her brother was molested by Father Paone …
>
> "Had I been aware of this allegation in Father Paone's past, I would not have supported his request for a priestly assignment in your diocese. Nor would I have written to you indicating that he was a priest in good standing."[4]

In other words, Dreher completely misinformed his audience. As soon as Wuerl had information on Paone's past, he immediately spread the word. He also urgently recalled Paone back to Pittsburgh to address the claims against him and sent him off to the St. Luke's inpatient treatment center in Maryland. Paone never had a parish assignment again.

(This author specifically informed Dreher of his erroneous information, yet he refused to correct it, and it still appears on his web site today continuing to deceive readers.)

Why did Catholic media go mute after the 2018 report? Well, a main reason is that in the years leading up to 2018, the presence of Catholic voices grew on social media platforms such as Twitter. But a result of this success was that a cowardice evolved. Catholic voices became deathly afraid of being attacked as a "Vatican flak" or "pedophile defender" if they dared to stick up for the Catholic Church.

Catholic voices began to operate on the principle that if they joined their secular counterparts in either attacking the Catholic Church on the abuse issue or just simply remaining completely silent, they would remain generally immune from negative mob attacks and preserve their Twitter followings.

Meanwhile, some Catholic voices saw Shapiro's grand jury report as an opportunity to attack bishops with whom they disagreed ideologically. Conservative-leaning forums went after prelates like Cardinal Wuerl, whom they did not perceive to be sufficiently orthodox in their thinking. The outcome of these attacks, however, was that these partisan platforms began airing stories that were simply false, and in some cases, quite bizarre.

For example, the conservative site Church Militant, operated by the histrionic Michael Voris, published a surreal story following the Pennsylvania report claiming that the grand jury had concluded that Cardinal Wuerl had paid "hush money" to an accused priest "in exchange for silence on other priests' criminal conduct."[5]

In truth, Shapiro's report said no such thing about "hush payments" of any kind, and the accused priest did not receive any money for "silence." In fact, documents released by the Diocese of Pittsburgh showed the exact opposite. When an accused priest (George Zirwas) wrote to the diocese asking for an increase in his stipend, the diocese merely informed the guy that if he had information related to abuse claims, he should come forward and report them. That's it. Church Militant's claim was false.[6]

But an especially surreal episode occurred one mid-afternoon just a couple weeks after Shapiro's report – on August 30. Whereas Church Militant would generally send emails to its supporters every morning about stories it had recently published, Michael Voris suddenly flooded the email inboxes of his followers in the middle of the afternoon with a message of extreme urgency.

"BREAKING NEWS EXCLUSIVE: Wuerl Bombshell" was the title of the important email, and Voris implored his readers to visit his web site and tune in to a critical report to be broadcast *live* a short time later (~5:15pm). And when that magic moment arrived, Voris stood in front of a camera and earnestly told his viewers:

> "Church Militant has learned from reliable sources that Pope Francis has directed Cardinal Donald Wuerl of Washington, D.C., be spirited out of the United States before Wuerl could possibly be arrested by U.S. federal authorities."

It was a shocking piece of news, indeed. One could envision Cardinal Wuerl with a trench coat over his head quietly ducking onto a private plane in the dark of night to be hurriedly whisked away overseas. Voris also claimed that Wuerl had "gone underground," "off the grid," and into complete hiding. "All public appearances have been canceled," Voris asserted.[7]

But Voris' "bombshell" turned out to be a bomb. His story was completely false. Within 72 hours of Voris' announcement reporting that Wuerl was in complete hiding and soon to be spirited off to the Vatican, Wuerl was actually presiding at a public Sunday Mass that was *broadcast on television*.[8] Not only was Wuerl not "off the grid" or "underground," he was still making public appearances, appearances that Voris said that Wuerl had canceled.

The false "Bombshell/Breaking News" report was a complete embarrassment for Church Militant. The group quietly deleted the video from its web site, yet it also wrote, "We stand by our reporting and have complete confidence in our sources."[9] Oh, boy.

Critical analysis of the 2018 Pennsylvania grand jury report was nearly absent across the entire Catholic media landscape.[10] However, in January 2019, four months after the report's release, Peter Steinfels, a former reporter with the *New York Times*, published a sweeping rejoinder to Shapiro's report in *Commonweal* magazine, "The PA Grand Jury Report: Not What It Seems: It's Inaccurate, Unfair & Misleading." It was an impressive work.

In a nutshell, Steinfels concluded that Josh Shapiro's incendiary charge that Catholic dioceses "brushed aside" "all" victims while leaders "did nothing" is "in fact grossly misleading, irresponsible, inaccurate, and unjust."

> "This ugly, indiscriminate, and inflammatory charge, unsubstantiated by the report's own evidence, to say nothing of the evidence the report ignores, is truly unworthy of a judicial body responsible for impartial justice."[11]

Steinfels' article was a valuable rebuttal. It was just unfortunate that it was published months after the report's release and long after the reputations of numerous priests were already irreparably destroyed.

On the afternoon of August 30, 2018, Michael Voris of Church Militant broadcast an urgent live "bombshell" news report claiming that Cardinal Donald W. Wuerl had gone into hiding and was about to be spirited off to the Vatican to avoid criminal prosecution. It was all untrue.

Oops: Less than 72 hours after Church Militant cited "reliable sources" in reporting that Cardinal Wuerl had "gone underground" and had "canceled all public appearances," Wuerl was presiding at a Sunday Mass on September 2, 2018, a public appearance broadcast on television.

Not even hiding the hate in Michigan

It is very easy to throw the term *anti-Catholic* at someone for merely criticizing the Catholic Church. The term loses its true meaning when it is applied recklessly.

But there are episodes when that label truly applies, when anti-Catholicism is surely at the root of someone's endeavor to investigate the Catholic Church.

Such has been the case in the state of Michigan.

When she was elected Attorney General in 2018, Dana Nessel became the first openly 'LGBTQ' candidate to win a statewide office. She had been a fierce advocate for gay marriage in the state and then married another woman. The pair reportedly have custody of two children.

When Nessel ran for office, she even touted the fact that she "didn't have a penis" as a primary reason to vote for her.[12]

Those facts alone gave pause as to whether Nessel might have some animus against the Church in light of its teachings on sexuality.

But questions about a possible animus were certainly answered at a press conference she conducted in February 2019 when she announced the continuation of a criminal investigation against the Catholic Church over allegations of abuse from many decades earlier. It was a remark from Nessel that left little doubt about where her mind was. Nessel announced:

"If an investigator comes to your door and asks to speak with you, please ask to see their badge and not their rosary."[13]

It was a disturbing remark, indeed. Obviously, a public official would never get away with such a clearly bigoted remark against another religion. If a law enforcement official investigating a Jewish group said, "If an investigator comes to your door and asks to speak with you, please ask to see their badge and not their yarmulke," the outrage would be rightfully swift and furious. That individual's career would be finished. Kaput.

Indeed, after her election it soon became clear that Nessel had it out for the Church. In a television interview, she even referred to the Church as a "criminal enterprise."[14]

A "criminal enterprise"?

According to government statistics, the Michigan cities of Detroit and Flint remain among the most violent big cities in the country. And multiple media outlets have reported about children all over the state being targeted for sickening sex acts.[15] Yet looking at AG Nessel's own Twitter feed, one can see where she has expended her energies, ruffling through files in search of possible abuse committed by priests not today, but many decades ago:

Dana Nessel ✔
@dananessel

These are some of the amazing volunteers from the Michigan Attorney General's office who spend each weekend sifting through hundreds of thousands of documents confiscated on the Catholic Church clergy abuse cases.

♡ 317   10:46 AM - May 5, 2019

In the 1950s, historian Arthur Schlesinger, Sr., called anti-Catholicism "the deepest-held bias in the history of the American people."[16] That was not only true then, but the bias has clearly become much, much worse.

NOTES

[1] For example: Jimmy Akin, "Smoking Gun Memo In Murphy Paedophilia Case!" *National Catholic Register* blog, April 5, 2010. https://www.ncregister.com/blog/jimmy-akin/smoking_gun_memo_in_murphy_paedophilia_case and Fr. Thomas T. Brundage, "Parts of the Fr. Murphy story you haven't read," *Catholic Herald*, March 31, 2010, https://catholicherald.org/news/local/parts-of-the-fr-murphy-story-you-havent-read/

[2] There are many examples. Some that came to mind for this author were: When the "documentary" film *Deliver Us From Evil* was released in 2006, Grant Gallicho wrote an effective response to the film at *Commonweal* magazine, November 6, 2006 ... Fr. Raymond J. de Souza, "A Response to the *New York Times*," *National Review*, March 27, 2010 ... Tim Drake, "Change in Vatican Culture: A Sex Abuse Expert Sees Hope in Pope Benedict," *National Catholic Register*, April 16, 2020.

[3] Rod Dreher, "The PA Catholic Sex Abuse Horror," August 14, 2018. Retrieved April 8, 2018, from https://www.theamericanconservative.com/dreher/the-pa-catholic-sex-abuse-horror/

[4] "Response for the Catholic Diocese of Pittsburgh to Report of the 40th Statewide Investigating Grand Jury," July/August 2018.

[5] Christine Niles, "PA Grand Jury: Cdl. Wuerl paid hush money to child porn priest," August 15, 2018.

https://www.churchmilitant.com/news/article/pa-grand-jury-cdl.-wuerl-paid-hush-money-to-child-porn-priest

6 "Response for the Catholic Diocese of Pittsburgh."

7 Church Militant, "Breaking News Exclusive: Wuerl Bombshell," August 30, 2018. https://www.churchmilitant.com/news/article/breaking-news-exclusive-wuerl-bombshell [Important note: Church Militant deleted the video from its web site, but the original is still posted on YouTube (as of April 2020), and this author is in possession of the original video.]

8 CNN video, September 2, 2018. Accessed April 2020 from https://www.youtube.com/watch?v=4xygnLnlsYA .

9 Church Militant, "Breaking News Exclusive: Wuerl Bombshell."

10 There are two exceptions. This author, writing at TheMediaReport.com, published an extensive, multi-part factual rebuttal to Shapiro's report. In addition, William A. Donohue of the Catholic League wrote a report, "Pennsylvania Grand Jury Report Debunked," August 16, 2018.

11 Peter Steinfels, "The PA Grand-Jury Report: Not What It Seems: It's Inaccurate, Unfair & Misleading," Commonweal, January 25, 2019. Accessed at https://www.commonwealmagazine.org/pa-grand-jury-report-not-what-it-seems

12 YouTube video, "Dana Nessel - Who can you count on not to show you their penis?" Accessed April 2020 from https://www.youtube.com/watch?v=GJdlPdqWmCc

13 Megan Banta, "Attorney General Nessel to Catholic Church: Stop self-policing," Lansing State Journal, February 21, 2019.

14 Ken Kolker, "AG: Priests, church leaders could face criminal charges," WOOD-TV (Channel 8, NBC affiliate, Grand Rapids, Michigan), February 15, 2019.

15 For example: Heather Catallo, "Man accused of 'sextorting' Michigan teens facing more charges," WXYZ-TV (ABC affiliate, Detroit, Michigan), April 30, 2019. Also: Trace Christenson, "Springfield woman in child rape and child porn ring enters plea," Battle Creek Enquirer, March 5, 2019.

[16] Attributed to historian Arthur Schlesinger, Sr., in the book by Msgr. John Tracy Ellis (1956). *American Catholics and the Intellectual Life* (The Heritage Foundation, Inc.). Referenced from: William A. Donohue, "Nothing Covert About Anti-Catholicism," The Catholic League, November 2002.

8

A Disastrous Practice

"No one would hold a brain surgeon to today's standard of care for professional decisions he made in 1970. Yet the decisions made in 1970 by Catholic bishops, who routinely consulted with mental health professionals about sick priests, are being judged by today's standards. Today, the confidence of the mental health community about the likelihood of curing sexual disorders is far less than it was in 1970."

– L. Martin Nussbaum[1]

"On countless occasions, psychologists gave bishops terrible advice about abusive priests – and, of course, this bad advice led to terrible consequences for victims and the broader church. Yet these psychologists have gotten off scot-free in the media."

– U.S. District Court Judge Patrick J. Schiltz[2]

In its reporting of the Catholic Church abuse story, the media has often taken harsh note of the Church's practice from decades ago of "shipping abusers off to treatment" when receiving word that a priest may have committed abuse.

Indeed, it is entirely *true* that when bishops were confronted with the news that a priest had abused, the bishop would often send that priest off to one of a handful of inpatient treatment centers around the country. At Church expense, a priest would spend weeks, and sometimes months, at these centers, and depending upon the recommendations of the doctors who treated the priest, a bishop would decide whether to send the priest back to full ministry, limited ministry, or none at all.

When viewed through today's lens, many look at this routine as unconscionable. "How on earth could bishops have done such a thing?" they ask. "How callous!" they exclaim. (Others have observed that some bishops did not fully invoke the Code of Canon Law, which, under Canon 1395 §2, states that a cleric who sexually abuses a person under 16 years of age "is to be punished with just penalties, not excluding dismissal from the clerical state if the case so warrants."[3])

However, despite how the media has portrayed it, the practice of sending abusive priests off to treatment was not some nefarious attempt to deflect responsibility and cover-up wrongdoing. It was a genuine attempt by bishops to *accept* responsibility and proactively address the problem they were confronted with.

While such a practice seems reckless today, the process of sending sexual abusers to treatment was not some aberration within the Catholic Church; it was a widespread routine within secular society as well. As Dr. Monica Applewhite, a longtime expert in prevention and response to sex abuse within organizations, has written:

> "From the 1950s to the 1980s, these treatment-based interventions for sexual criminals were not only enormously prevalent in the United States, but surveys of ordinary citizens

showed that they were enormously popular.

"[T]he science of human sexuality and sexual offending is extraordinarily young. Virtually all of the information we utilize today regarding the treatment and supervision of sexual offenders has been discovered since 1985."[4]

Indeed, when one looks at media accounts of sex crimes from past decades, one sees that modest prison terms and "court-ordered therapy" were common sentences in the criminal justice system in the United States.

For example, in 1977, police in Revere, Massachusetts, rounded up nearly two dozen men for having sex with as many as *63* young boys over a period of four years.[5] The men, some of whom reportedly flew in from other areas of the country to commit their crimes, enticed the boys by offering them marijuana, beer, and cash.[6] Criminal charges against the men included rape, sodomy, "indecent assault and battery on a child under 14," and "unnatural acts with a child under 14."[7] Tragically, many of the boys were already from broken homes,[8] and some were foster children under the care of the state.[9] When all the cases finally made their way through the system, almost none of the perpetrators saw the inside of a prison cell. Rather, a judge sentenced most of them to mere *probation* and therapy.[10]

In 1978, when a criminal jury in Boston took only 90 minutes to convict Donald M. Allen, a 51-year-old prominent psychiatrist and former instructor at Harvard Medical School, on four counts of rape of a 15 year-old boy, a judge sentenced Dr. Allen to a modest five years' probation "on the condition he undergoes psychiatric treatment."[11] The *Boston Globe* then reported how both judges and trial lawyers *praised* the jurist's decision, with one fellow judge calling the sentence "eminently fair."[12]

It is important to note that bishops not only acted with the best of intentions when sending abusive priests off to treatment, but they also did so because a 1985 report written directly to them specifically instructed that they do this very thing.

In June 1985, a trio of men issued a report to all American bishops entitled, "The Problem of Sexual Molestation by Roman Catholic Clergy: Meeting the Problem in a Comprehensive and Responsible Manner." It had been written on the heels of the first nationally renowned story of sex abuse by a Catholic priest, the notorious case of Gilbert Gauthe in Louisiana. The three men who authored the report were:

- Rev. Thomas P. Doyle, a Dominican priest and canon lawyer;
- F. Ray Mouton, Jr., a defense lawyer who had defended Gauthe; and
- Rev. Michael R. Peterson, a priest-psychologist who had founded St. Luke Institute, a psychiatric hospital in Silver Spring Maryland and a treatment center for abusive and troubled clergy.

The trio convened to write the report to address what they rightly believed to be a glaring and growing problem in the Church. Rev. Doyle has since admitted that Boston's Cardinal Bernard Law was an early ally of the group report.[13]

What did the report say? For starters, the report correctly noted that the Church was facing a major crisis. Catholic priests had abused children, and there was colossal harm being wreaked upon victims as well as the Church.

The 92-page report also aptly observed that American

society had changed in its litigiousness in recent years. For example, whereas there was once a time when suing a doctor was unthinkable, malpractice lawsuits had now become commonplace. This change in the culture had serious implications for the Catholic Church, the report correctly indicated. The trio also accurately noted that contingency lawyers clearly had the Catholic Church in their crosshairs.

However, a major component of the report was providing bishops the steps they should take in dealing with abusive priests on both the pastoral and legal levels.

Most notably, the trio wholeheartedly believed that many priests who abused children could indeed return to active ministry following psychological treatment. (Years later, civil and canon lawyer Nicholas P. Cafardi would write that the report was an "unabashed endorsement of the therapeutic approach to the problem of clergy sexual abuse of minors."[14])

In a supplemental chapter to the trio's 1985 report, Rev. Peterson would write, "These are lifelong diseases for which there is now *much hope for recovery and control of the disorders*" (italics added).

As remarkable as seems today, the authors of the 1985 actually believed, as many psychologists did at the time, that, although there was not a *cure*, there could be "recovery and control" for abusive pedophiles. Peterson also added:

> "It is a fact that treatment can help rehabilitate clerics so that they may return to active ministry in most instances irregardless [*sic*] of jail time or no legal complications."[15]

It's true. Peterson clearly believed and advocated that priests who abused kids, if properly "treated," could most certainly return to active ministry, even if they had served time in prison or been sued!

Decades later, we all know that this advice was essentially disastrous. But it must be stressed again that such therapeutic treatments were widely embraced in the secular culture and in the media. No less than the *Boston Globe* and the *New York Times* were trumpeting such treatments as late as 1992. A front-page article in the *Boston Globe* on Thursday, June 18, 1992, opened (bold added):

> "A new generation of treatment programs for sex offenders is proving **highly effective**, dramatically reducing the percentage of cases in which offenders repeat sex crimes, research shows.
>
> "Recidivism rates declined from 9 percent for untreated offenders to 5 percent for those who underwent the new treatment in one study, and from 38 percent to 6 percent in another.
>
> "While there is no complete 'cure' for sex offenders, **the new findings indicate that many of them can learn to manage their aberrant sexual impulses without committing new crimes**. The promising new treatments focus on helping these offenders control the complex cauldron of social inadequacies, distorted thinking, and deviant sex fantasies that prompt them to rape women, molest children or exhibit themselves in public."[16]

A similar article in the *New York Times* ("Giving Healing and Hope to Priests Who Molested") aired a similar tone.[17]

Remarkably, even as recently as the mid-1990s – when the media coverage of the Catholic Church abuse story continued to swell – surveys showed that a significant number of Catholics actually supported the therapeutic approach for abusive priests.

In his 1996 book, *A Tragic Grace: The Catholic Church and Child Sexual Abuse*, priest-psychologist Msgr. Stephen J. Rossetti polled 1,810 Catholics on their agreement with the following scenario: "I would accept a former priest-child abuser into *my parish* if he had undergone psychological treatment and was being supervised by another priest." A majority of respondents – although slight, 51% – *agreed* with the statement while only 22% disagreed. Twenty-seven percent were "unsure."[18] It is inconceivable that anything other than a low single-digit percentage would agree with such a statement nowadays.

Times have changed dramatically.

New therapy seen to cut repeat sex crimes

By Alison Bass
GLOBE STAFF

went the new treatment in one study, and from 38 percent to 6 percent in another.

equacies, distorted thinking, and deviant sex fantasies that prompt them to rape women, molest chil-

An offender's right to treatment...

Ways cited to treat priests who abuse

By James L. Franklin
GLOBE STAFF

Above: In its 2002 blitzkrieg against the Catholic Church, the Boston Globe *lambasted the Catholic Church for sending abusive priests off to treatment. But apparently the* Globe *forgot that only ten years earlier, they themselves were trumpeting such treatments in their own paper as* **"highly effective"** *and* **"dramatic."**
(Images from the Boston Globe, *top to bottom: June 18, 1992; June 26, 1992; July 19, 1992)*

Below: A similar article touting treatment for abusive priests appeared in the New York Times *on October 12, 1992:*

A11 L
THE NEW YORK TIMES **NATIONAL** MONDAY, OCTOBER 12, 1992

Giving Healing and Hope to Priests Who Molested

A light on *Spotlight*

In 2015, the Catholic Church sex abuse story exploded in the media yet again with the release of the Hollywood film *Spotlight*, a dramatization of the *Boston Globe*'s work leading up to its 2002 publication of stories about the Catholic Church. (This author once calculated that in the 2002 year alone, the *Boston Globe* published 947 items related to the Catholic Church abuse story, a rate of over two-and-a-half items *per day*.[19])

However, like everything that comes out of Hollywood, the truth was lost along the way. (This author composed a lengthy rebuttal to the film at TheMediaReport.com and also published the book *Sins of the Press: The Untold Story of The Boston Globe's Reporting on Sex Abuse in the Catholic Church*.)

Yet there is one episode in particular that took place after the release of *Spotlight* that underscores how honesty and fairness were not a priority for the filmmakers as well as the writers at the *Globe* who were portrayed in the movie.

At least four people spoke out after the release of the film complaining that they had been falsely portrayed. One of those men was Jack Dunn, who was a trustee at Boston College High School ("BC High") during the time period of the film. The film contains a scene depicting *Globe* writers having a contentious meeting with Dunn at BC High, and in the scene Dunn acts callous and dismissive to abuse claims lodged against a priest at his school.

At one point in the scene, Dunn's character addresses *Boston Globe* writer Walter Robinson ("Robby") and says, "It's a big school, Robby, you know that. And we're talking about seven alleged victims over, what, eight years?"

Dunn strongly objected to this portrayal of him, saying that the characterization was not only the opposite of how the meeting transpired but also of how he addressed cases of abusive priests at his school. In truth, Dunn was incredibly proactive in his handling of the issue.

Dunn was so upset upon seeing such a depiction of him in the movie that after he exited the theater, he vomited onto the sidewalk. "I'm portrayed in the exact opposite manner regarding what I did, said and feel," Dunn told the *Boston Herald*. "They manufactured dialogue because they needed a villain, and they chose apparently to make me a villain."[20]

Dunn hired lawyers to demand that the film's distributors remove the offending scene from the film.

But the filmmakers pushed back, claiming that Dunn was "accurately characterized" in the movie and that the two *Globe* writers who were at the actual meeting – Walter Robinson and Sacha Pfeiffer – could substantiate and affirm that the depicted scene was truthful.

Robinson, who himself was an alumnus of BC High, publicly declared that the scene was indeed faithful to the truth, claiming that the real-life encounter "was a very painful interview for me to do, at an institution which I remain very close to. So I remember it quite well."[21]

Dunn began his crusade to clear his name in November 2015, not long after the release of the film. As the beginning of 2016 arrived, *Spotlight* began receiving international recognition and winning major awards. On February 23, 2016, *Spotlight* was released for sale on DVD and BluRay disc. And the evening of February 28, 2016, was a big night for the film, as *Spotlight* took home coveted Academy Awards, including Best Original Screenplay and Best Picture.[22]

The reason for mentioning the dates and awards is important, because it was on March 15, 2016, the producers of *Spotlight* issued a public statement admitting that the dialogue attributed to Dunn in the film was fictional and that the film mischaracterized what Dunn did and said as a trustee at BC High. As part of a settlement, the producers agreed to make donations in Dunn's name to local charities that Dunn had chosen.[23]

"I feel exonerated, but it will not erase the devastating experience of being falsely portrayed in a film," Dunn said after he was vindicated.[24]

What the producers did was quite devious. It was not until *after their film won all its awards and collected its loot from DVD/BluRay sales* that they finally acknowledged that what they did was wrong. They smeared an innocent man, but they wouldn't admit it until after they collected all the award statues and dollars that they could.

And remember: The *Globe*'s own Walter Robinson – speaking on behalf of both himself and colleague Sacha Pfeiffer – had publicly claimed that the scene depicting Dunn was indeed faithful and that he had remembered the original encounter "quite well."

"It was a not-atypical encounter between a reporter with tough questions and a public relations representative who is doing his very best to minimize the damage that is going to be done to his institution in what is clearly going to be an unhappy story," Robinson had said. "That's what happened in 2002, and that's what the scene is about."[25]

Now we know that was all a lie.

NOTES

[1] L. Martin Nussbaum, "Changing the Rules," *America* (magazine), May 15, 2006.

[2] Patrick J. Schiltz, "Not all the news is fit to print: What the media missed in the sexual-abuse scandal," *Commonweal*, August 15, 2003.

[3] Code of Canon Law, Can. 1395 §2,
https://www.vatican.va/archive/ENG1104/_P56.HTM

[4] Monica Applewhite, "Address of Dr. Monica Applewhite to the Irish Bishops, March 10, 2009," retrieved from http://www.themediareport.com/wp-content/uploads/2012/11/Applewhite-Ireland-Address-Bishops-2009.pdf April 2020.

[5] "17th arrest made in child sex probe," *The Boston Globe*, December 11, 1977, p. 58.

[6] Ibid.

[7] Richard Connolly, Arthur Jones, "Police say operation Revere-based," *The Boston Globe*, December 9, 1977.

[8] "17th arrest."

[9] Richard J. Connolly, Arthur Jones, "State to decide aid for sex-ring victims," *The Boston Globe*, December 10, 1977, p. 3.
[Joseph McCain was a veteran Boston detective who discovered the sex ring. A biographer of McCain later told about McCain's experiences with the Revere cases, "Even with all the murderers and bad guys that he put away, [McCain] would go home at night, kiss his wife, walk the dog and sleep like a baby. But when it came to these well-heeled guys, with the imprimatur of upper-crust society, secretly molesting children, it sickened him so that he could not sleep." David Mehegan, "Book him: Regular guy as crime fighter," *The New York Times*, March 18, 2005.]

[10] Alan Sheehan, "12 child-sex cases decided in Suffolk," *The Boston Globe*, April 24, 1979, p. 21.

[11] Paul Langer, "Dr. Allen guilty, is given probation," *The Boston Globe*, December 23, 1978, p. 1.

[12] Joseph Harvey, "Doctor's sentence called fair," *The Boston Globe*, December 23, 1978, p. 20.

[13] Kristen Lombardi, "Failure to Act," *The Boston Phoenix*, October 4, 2001.

[14] Nicholas P. Cafardi (2008). *Before Dallas: The U.S. Bishops' Response to Clergy Sexual Abuse of Children*. New York: Paulist Press. p. 52.

[15] Rev. Michael R. Peterson, M.D., "Guidelines," December 9, 1985.

[16] Alison Bass, "New therapy seen to cut repeat sex crimes," *The Boston Globe*, June 18, 1992, p. 1.

[17] Peter Steinfels, "Giving Healing and Hope to Priests Who Molested," *The New York Times*, October 12, 1992, p. A11.

[18] Stephen J. Rossetti (1996). *A Tragic Grace: The Catholic Church and Child Sexual Abuse*. Collegeville, Minnesota: The Liturgical Press, p. 93.

[19] David F. Pierre, Jr. *Double Standard: Abuse Scandals and the Attack on the Catholic Church*. (Mattapoisett, MA: TheMediaReport.com), 2011, p. 22.

[20] Jack Encarnacao, "'Spotlight' injustices claimed," *The Boston Herald*, November 23, 2015. https://www.bostonherald.com/2015/11/23/spotlight-injustices-claimed/

[21] Evan Allen, "'Spotlight' filmmakers defend portrayal of BC spokesman," BostonGlobe.com, November 25, 2015.

[22] The film was an obvious success, although its domestic box office of $45 million was somewhat modest considering it was such a highly acclaimed film. It is one of the lowest grossing Best Picture winners of all time. (Boxofficemojo.com)

[23] "'Spotlight' producers vindicate BC spokesman" (Boston College news release), March 15, 2016. accessed from https://www.bc.edu/bc-web/bcnews/campus-community/announcements/spotlight-statement-vindicates-jack-dunn.html in April 2020.

[24] Mark Shanahan, "'Spotlight' studio acknowledges dialogue attributed to Jack Dunn was fiction," *The Boston Globe*, March 15, 2016.

[25] Evan Allen.

9

Buffalo Bias

In recent decades, in an effort to boost sagging ratings, local television stations have employed "investigative reporters" to pump out highly charged stories that expose societal wrongdoing, whether it be crooked local businesses or corrupt government employees. These specialized reporters play a powerful role at the station in that they present an image to the public that the station is a trusted force for good in the community. At their best, these reporters do indeed give a voice to those who would otherwise have no voice at all.

But then there is Charlie Specht of WKBW-TV in Buffalo, an investigative reporter who has used his influence to exploit the issue of abuse by priests and unfairly attack the Catholic Church. In 2018, Specht began airing a blizzard of stories about decades-old allegations against Buffalo priests, often in the most sensationalized manner that he could muster. But viewers soon took notice that Specht was not being honest with his audience.

On a night in October 2018, Specht aired a story featuring an accuser who had only recently come forward to claim that a Buffalo priest had groped him outside an area Walmart "in the 1980s."[1] It was a troubling charge, indeed.

But one eagle-eyed viewer, a longtime resident of the area, saw Specht's report and did not remember there even being a Walmart in the area in the 1980s. He was right. After some quick research, he learned that Walmart did not even open its first store in the entire state of New York until 1991, and the first Walmart did not open in the Buffalo area until April of 1995, a far cry from the 1980s.

Would a discrepancy like this disprove the accuser's allegation? Not necessarily, but many would say it would. But what was most bothersome was how Charlie Specht responded when confronted with the factual problem of the accuser's allegation. When the viewer emailed Specht and questioned him about the existence of a Walmart in the 1980s, Specht confidently replied back to the viewer, "[Y]es I did check and it did exist back then."

But there was simply no way that Specht could have checked whether a Walmart existed in the Buffalo area in the 1980s. If he did, he would easily have learned that there were no Walmarts anywhere in all of New York state in the 1980s. Multiple sources confirmed the viewer's suspicion.[2]

There is no other conclusion to reach except that Specht lied to the viewer who wrote to him.

It was not until January 2020 that Specht publicly admitted in a radio interview that there was indeed no Walmart in the 1980s and that the accuser was now stating that the location of him being groped was an Ames store.[3] But Specht didn't explain how the accuser mistook a Walmart superstore for an Ames store. Specht has also allowed the erroneous information to remain on WKBW's web site to this day.[4]

Busted lying: A viewer questioned WKBW's Charlie Specht about an allegation that a priest groped a man outside a Walmart "in the 1980s." In fact, there was no Walmart anywhere in the Buffalo area until 1995. Yet Specht replied to the viewer that he "did check" about the existence of the Walmart, and it did exist. This was a lie.

Another troubling aspect of Specht's coverage was his disparate treatment of accused Catholic priests whose cases were investigated and were found to be innocent. And this disparate treatment may have been based on his station's long relationship with a lawyer who was actually once a reporter at his station.

In January of 2020, Charlie Specht aired a report on two accused Buffalo priests who had been exonerated and returned to ministry (Fr. Roy Herberger and Msgr. Fred Leising). The segment contained some predictable cheap shots at the Church by Specht, but it was generally a sympathetic piece of two priests who went through the agonizing ordeal of being falsely accused. Fair enough.

Yet when Specht reported the case of Fr. Dennis Riter, a parish priest from St. Elizabeth Ann Seton Church in Dunkirk, New York, southwest of Buffalo, he adopted a totally different tone. Just as with the other two priests Specht had reported on, investigators found Riter to be completely innocent, and the diocese returned him to his parish. But rather than portraying the case as the clear bogus accusation that it was, Specht reported the story as one of the diocese recklessly returning a priest to active ministry "despite abuse claims." For good measure, Specht also quoted some random alleged Catholic as saying, "I think it's absolutely disgusting," that the exonerated priest was returned to ministry.[5]

And in subsequent stories, Specht continued to depict the case as one in which the Buffalo Diocese had callously returned an abusive priest to ministry. Specht trumpeted the claim that the diocese's decision to return Rev. Riter to ministry was "outrageous, reckless, hazardous, and dangerous, and it poses a real and continuing threat to the safety of the children in the Diocese of Buffalo and in the [local] community."[6]

It was a curious disparity that raised a question: Why did Specht so clearly side with the accuser and his attorneys and against the Buffalo Diocese in his reporting of this particular case? Well, it turned out that one of the accuser's attorneys was a lawyer named Steve Boyd, who was once a *reporter at a Charlie Specht's station.*

In the years before he became a licensed lawyer, Steve Boyd worked in the 1990s as an investigative reporter at WKBW, the very same station as Specht. And just like Specht, Boyd worked the Catholic sex abuse beat doing several stories about the Catholic Church.

And there's more. In August of 2019, Boyd appeared as a guest on WKBW's mid-morning *AM Buffalo* program. One of Boyd's clients sat next to him, and the program's host asked Boyd about recent legislation that had been passed in New York that enabled people to sue the Catholic Church for abuse claims, no matter how long ago the alleged abuse occurred. The interview was a grand opportunity for Boyd to drum up more clients to sue the Catholic Church. His name, office, and phone number appeared prominently on the screen during his 6 minute and 40 second interview.

But while *AM Buffalo* is categorized "News" program in WKBW's listings, undoubtedly unbeknownst to many viewers, Steve Boyd actually *paid* WKBW for his appearance on the program. It was not until the last 27 seconds of the interview that a screen with Boyd's picture and phone number suddenly informed the audience that Boyd's appearance was indeed a "Sponsored segment."

How much did Boyd dole out for his appearance on *AM Buffalo*? WKBW has never divulged that information. But it became apparent that Boyd's relationship with WKBW may have been affecting its coverage of abuse cases and resulting in disparate treatment by reporter Specht.

This author sent an email to Charlie Specht seeking a response to his disparate treatment of accused priests. In his reply, Specht strangely claimed that Fr. Riter's accuser was *not in fact* represented by Steve Boyd. It was truly a bizarre statement to make when one could plainly see that Boyd's name, office, and signature appear on the accuser's lawsuit against the Diocese of Buffalo.[7]

Did Specht lie to this author? This author hopes not. But Specht wouldn't explain his claim that Boyd did not represent

Fr. Riter's accuser when Boyd's signature was clearly on his lawsuit.

Buffalo reporter Charlie Specht claimed that lawyer Steve Boyd, a former reporter at Specht's station, did not represent an accuser of Fr. Dennis Riter. Yet Boyd's name and signature were on the accuser's lawsuit.

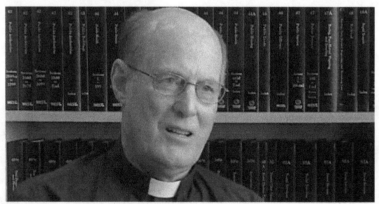

Rest In Peace: Falsely accused Buffalo priest Fr. Dennis Riter passed away in February 2020.

A tale of three innocent priests

In August of 2019, Buffalo's Charlie Specht of WKBW-TV wrote on Twitter to his followers:

Charlie Specht
@Charlie_Reports

Wow. Rev. Roy Herberger accused in a new CVA lawsuit. The @BuffaloDiocese exonerated him from previous allegation in December. (He maintained innocence). That makes THREE currently active priests under @BishopRJMalone who have been accused of sexually abusing minors today.

♡ 16   12:16 PM - Aug 14, 2019   ⓘ

  See Charlie Specht's other Tweets   ›

Yet it later turned out that **_all three_** of the priests to whom Specht referred were completely innocent.

Fr. Roy Herberger's accuser claimed that the priest had abused him at St. Ann's Parish and school in Buffalo in the 1980s. But not only did Herberger not have any connection to St. Ann's until 30 years later, but there was no record at all of the accuser even having attended there.

And quite remarkably, when a diocesan investigator asked the accuser where he attended elementary school, the accuser claimed that he couldn't remember. This prompted the investigator to write in his report to the diocesan review board, "It is not believable that someone would be completely unable to remember what elementary school he attended."[8] Indeed.

In the end, the investigation concluded that Fr. Herberger's case was not just one where the facts did not add up, but the accuser's wild claims of repeated acts of sodomy and oral sex were so implausible that it was literally "impossible for it to have happened."[9]

Meanwhile, Herberger's personal attorney also did some digging of his own and found that the accuser already had a criminal background that included a charge of falsifying documents.

And what about Herberger's "previous allegation" that Specht referred to in his tweet? It was the *same guy*. Even though the accuser had been completely discredited, he continued to seek a cash settlement under New York's Child Victims Act, a state law passed in 2019 which allowed individuals to sue the Catholic Church no matter how long ago they say their abuse occurred.

As far as the other two priests referred to in Specht's tweet, Monsignor Peter J. Popadick and the Rev. Paul M. Nogaro (who was already retired), both had several decades of unblemished ministries without any accusations until a troubled man in his 60s came forward to claim that *four* priests as well as *two* Catholic grade school teachers had raped him between the ages of 10 and 11, a scope of abuse which no reasonable person would believe.[10]

The accuser also refused to speak to investigators about his allegations or submit any sworn testimony about what he was claiming.

In reporting to his audience that Msgr. Popadick and Fr. Nagaro had been reinstated, Specht reported nothing about the accuser's implausible claim of having been abused by a total of *six* individuals within two years and that the accusations surely appeared to be the machinations of a disturbed person.

Rather, in his report about the two priests being exonerated, Specht turned to a longtime Church critic and local "victim advocate" to excoriate the Church on how it conducted its investigations.[11]

NOTES

[1] Charlie Specht, "Buffalo Diocese seminary blamed for sexual culture among priests," WKBW, October 28, 2018. Retrieved from https://www.wkbw.com/news/i-team/buffalo-diocese-seminary-blamed-for-sexual-culture-among-priests , accessed April 2020.

[2] Research into the opening dates of Walmart stores across the United States (accessed August 2019):
- Thomas J. Holmes, University of Minnesota, http://users.econ.umn.edu/~holmes/data/WalMart/ …
- Also: https://github.com/cjbayesian/walmart/blob/master/data/store_ope nings.csv …
- https://walmartmuseum.auth.cap-hosting.com/timeline/decades/1990

[3] TheMediaReport.com, "Comin' Clean: Buffalo Reporter Admits to Errors In His Reporting," January 13, 2020. Retrieved from http://www.themediareport.com/2020/01/13/buffalo-specht-false-report/

[4] Specht, October 28, 2018.

[5] Charlie Specht, "With Buffalo diocese in crisis, Bishop Malone goes on vacation: Fr. Dennis Riter exonerated despite abuse claims," WKBW, June 29, 2018.

[6] Charlie Specht, "Attorneys press Bishop Malone for answers on

Father Riter controversy," WKBW, July 2, 2018. Accessed from
https://www.wkbw.com/news/attorneys-press-bishop-malone-for-answers-on-father-riter-controversy April 2020.

[7] TheMediaReport.com, "SPECIAL REPORT: Scandal at WKBW-TV In Buffalo: Contingency Lawyer Buys Airtime, and His Client Gets the Kid-Glove Treatment by Station," April 22, 2020.

[8] Daniel Telvock, "How a priest got cleared of sexual abuse allegations," WIVB-TV, November 11, 2019. Accessed https://www.wivb.com/news/how-a-priest-got-cleared-of-sexual-abuse-allegations/ April 2020.

[9] Ibid.

[10] Lou Michel, "Two Buffalo Diocese priests accused of sex abuse returned to ministry," *Buffalo News*, January 17, 2020.

[11] Charlie Specht, "Buffalo Diocese reinstates two priests accused of child sexual abuse," WKBW-TV, January 17, 2020. Accessed from https://www.wkbw.com/news/i-team/buffalo-diocese-reinstates-two-priests-accused-of-child-sexual-abuse.

10

The Story Behind the Story in Buffalo

When a tsunami of stories about the Diocese of Buffalo began to air in 2018, people in Buffalo understandably believed that the narrative was one of Bishop Richard Malone allowing known child predators to continue in ministry. Indeed, this was the very story that Charlie Specht and the rest of the Buffalo media led the public to believe.

In truth, however, not a single priest in Buffalo who had a substantiated accusation of abuse against a minor remained in active ministry. The "crisis" in Buffalo had almost *nothing* whatsoever to do with children. In truth, the real story in Buffalo was about active homosexual priests lashing out at Bishop Malone in the media in an effort to save their own priesthoods. While this may appear like a crazy conspiracy theory, the facts bear out the reality.

In September 2019, Rev. Ryszard Biernat, the personal assistant to Bishop Malone, created a local media firestorm after he secretly recorded his boss for several months and then released selectively chosen tapes to the media. The media predictably framed the story as Biernat being a "whistleblower" uncovering wrongdoing by his bishop.

However, Biernat's audio recordings revealed nothing more than Bishop Malone occasionally despairing over the negative media coverage that he was receiving. Biernat's actions were an enormous betrayal of his boss that served no other purpose except to publicly embarrass Malone, although the media naturally did not report it as such.

What the media also failed to tell the public was that Biernat had a clear ulterior motivation for recording his bishop. Before coming out as a "whistleblower," Rev. Biernat was found to be in an intimate homosexual relationship with a young seminarian named Matthew Bojanowski. The two lovers had even bought a house together. Months before Biernat released his audio recordings, a steamy love letter that Biernat had written three years earlier to Bojanowski surfaced. The letter was truly embarrassing, as it exposed two gay men living in clear violation of their vow of celibacy. In the letter dated July 13, 2016, Biernat wrote to Bojanowski:

> "Remember? The library of the bishop's house? ... What I have been feeling for you is something totally new and different from all the other feelings of love I have experienced ... I have no hesitations in saying that I love you ... I will always love you more than yesterday ...
>
> "I will always love you, and if you leave, I'll be O.K. ... At this point, I cannot imagine my life without you ...
>
> "So my beloved Matthew, I hope and pray that you are my 'other 1/2 that walks life's journey with' me!! Forever grateful for loving me first!"[1]

The Story Behind the Story in Buffalo

In full context, it is now understandable why Biernat felt the necessity to become a "whistleblower." The reason to secretly record Malone was to detract public attention from his love affair and salvage his own priesthood.

Needless to say, Buffalo media – forever on the side of anyone in opposition to Bishop Malone – did not report on Biernat's letter honestly. TV reporter Charlie Specht tried to minimize and downplay the steamy letter by characterizing it as merely "platonic."[2] The *Buffalo News* even once tried to tell readers it was only "an expression of friendship."[3]

And Siobhan O'Connor, a close friend of Fr. Biernat and a former diocesan employee who attracted widespread media attention after stealing documents from the diocese, claimed on her personal blog that the romantic love letter was somehow not even a romantic love letter. "I do not believe it is a love letter," O'Connor wrote.[4]

Buffalo's Rev. Ryszard Biernat (r) having fun at the beach with seminarian Matthew Bojanowski (l)

WKBW's lead story

At Charlie Specht's WKBW-TV in Buffalo, it soon became apparent that when it came to reporting on the Catholic Church, perspective and fairness were not a priority.

Emblematic of this fact was an episode in August 2019 in which a diocesan-employee-turned-"whistleblower," Siobhan O'Connor, and a former seminary dean, Stephen Parisi, staged a "rally" to demand the resignation of Bishop Richard Malone.

Yet when it came time for the highly touted rally, a whopping *three* people showed up – and that included O'Connor and Parisi. Yet the paltry turnout did not stop WKBW from making the historic gathering of the trio the *lead item* on its nightly newscast.[5]

A three-person "rally" was the lead story on WKBW-TV in Buffalo.

NOTES

[1] TheMediaReport.com, "EXCLUSIVE: Buffalo's Bare-Chested Buddies: The Secret Love Letter the Media is Hiding," September 11, 2019. http://www.themediareport.com/2019/09/11/exclusive-biernat-bojanowski-love-letter-buffalo/

[2] Charlie Specht, "I-TEAM: Bishop Malone accused of 'cover-up' with active Buffalo Diocese priest," WKBW-TV, August 6, 2019.

[3] Dan Herbeck and Jay Tokasz, "Who is Father Ryszard Biernat, and why would he secretly record Bishop Malone?" *Buffalo News*, September 6, 2019.

[4] Siobhan O'Connor, "The Letter" (blog post), September 6, 2019. Accessed from https://respectfulcatholic.com/2019/09/06/the-letter/ April 2020.

[5] Taylor Epps, "Protesters call on Bishop Malone to resign," WKBW-TV, August 18, 2019. Retrieved from https://www.wkbw.com/news/local-news/protesters-call-on-bishop-malone-to-resign in April 2020.

11

When the Truth Is Also Victimized

It must be repeated that in addressing the topic of Catholic priest sex abuse committed decades ago, the suffering of victims must always be acknowledged. The agony of the immense betrayal and violation that criminal priests committed is all too real.

So what is one to make of the situation when a genuine victim of clergy abuse appears to have lied about how the Church handled his case?

On Tuesday, June 18, 2019, 50-year-old James Bottlinger stood with his attorneys in a Buffalo conference room in front of a row of television cameras and reporters. Bottlinger announced to the world that he had been abused as a teenager by Fr. Michael R. Freeman in the mid-1980s at St. Mary of the Assumption Parish in Lancaster, New York, in the Diocese of Buffalo.

Bottlinger claimed that at age 19, a few years after his abuse stopped, he was approached by a Church official who was investigating Freeman, and Bottlinger told the official of his abuse. But according to Bottlinger and his attorneys at their press conference, Church officials "really didn't do anything" and "Freeman was allowed to continue in ministry unabated and allowed to go into other parishes in Pennsylvania and other states."[1]

To the media, this was simply yet another cut-and-dry case of abuse and cover-up by the Catholic Church, just like the thousands of others that had been reported. Within minutes, Bottlinger's story was spread across the media landscape that the Catholic Church had failed yet again in stopping a serial molester.

Yet Bottlinger was not telling the truth, and it appears that Bottlinger and his lawyers knew this when they held their press conference. Church records reveal that on March 21, 1989, the Church completely revoked the faculties of Freeman and completely removed him from ministry. And if Bottlinger spoke to a diocesan official about his abuse at age 19, as he explicitly claimed, then Freeman would have been permanently removed from ministry soon after Bottlinger reported his abuse!

In fact, Freeman's very last assignment in the Church was at the parish where Bottlinger says Freeman abused him. And contrary to the claims of Bottlinger and his attorneys, this was Freeman's last assignment anywhere in the Church.

At the press conference, Bottlinger also claimed that he had learned from the 2018 Pennsylvania grand jury report that Freeman had continued on in ministry as a priest in Pennsylvania after abusing him. Yet in truth, the grand jury report *said no such thing at all* about Freeman continuing to work in Pennsylvania.[2]

Bottlinger's charges that Church officials "really didn't do anything" and that "Freeman was allowed to continue in ministry unabated" were completely false, and it is almost impossible to imagine that he and his attorneys did not know this. The facts of Freeman's ministry were not only clearly outlined in the previous year's Pennsylvania grand jury report but also in a report that one of Bottlinger's own lawyers published about accused priests in Buffalo months earlier![3]

There is no other conclusion to reach except that Bottlinger and his lawyers lied at their press conference. And such a charge cannot be made lightly.

Yet there was very little worry that the media would call out Bottlinger and his lawyers for their dishonesty, especially the media in Buffalo. It turned out that one of Bottlinger's lawyers was Steve Boyd; yes, the former reporter at WKBW and close ally of reporter Charlie Specht.

NOTES

[1] The video of Jeff Bottlinger's press conference can be seen at https://www.facebook.com/AndersonAdvocates/videos/26005375866 23081/ (accessed April 2020)

[2] TheMediaReport.com, "Greedy Jeff Anderson Holds Press Conference To Lie About Diocese's Handling of Abuse Case," June 24, 2019.

[3] Anderson Advocates, "Clerical Sexual Abuse in the Diocese of Buffalo Volume II," accessed April 2020 from https://www.andersonadvocates.com/Documents/posts/Report_Cleri cal_Sexual_Abuse_in_the_Diocese_of_Buffalo_Vol._2.pdf

12

The Catholic ATM

In the same way when someone walks up to an ATM and expects it to give him cash, it is now the same with the Catholic Church.

Comparing the Catholic Church to an ATM may appear like a crude comparison, but the analogy is apt. When a person sues the Catholic Church, that person has nothing to lose, yet a lot to possibly gain.

When a Catholic diocese is served with a lawsuit, it essentially has only two options:

1) Settle the case, or

2) Fight the lawsuit in a courtroom in front of a jury.

But as anyone who has had to go to court for a trial will tell you, court cases are expensive. It is easy to imagine a court case involving Catholic sex abuse, with multiple attorneys, witnesses, and dozens (if not hundreds) of hours of preparation, easily costing $200,000.

And while a criminal case requires a prosecutor prove a defendant guilty "beyond a reasonable doubt," the standard is far lower for a civil case. In a case of someone suing the Catholic Church, the plaintiff would only have to prove that the Church was negligent with 51% certainty in order to prevail.

With this lower standard of proof, it is no mystery as to why the Church chooses to settle nearly every case it is confronted with.

There are other factors as well. With the constant stream of Catholic priest sex abuse stories in the media dating back to the 1980s, it would be difficult for the Church to overcome the overwhelming public prejudice against it. Indeed, the criminal sex abuse committed by priests decades ago was sickening, and public anger is justified. But public sentiment would be a near-impossible hurdle a diocese to overcome in a public trial.

Another factor would be the negative media coverage if a diocese ever sought to defend itself in a case publicly. Even if the abuse accusation against a priest were provably bogus, there are writers at the Associated Press, the *Boston Globe*, the *New York Times*, the *Washington Post*, and other media outlets who would salivate at the opportunity to write articles portraying the big, bad Catholic Church as "forcing a victim to relive his abuse in a public courtroom."

Take the case involving Fr. Richard Donahue of the Archdiocese of Boston, a priest who up until 2017 and nearly a *half century* in the priesthood had a completely unblemished record. In 2017, a 55-year-old man sued the Archdiocese of Boston claiming that Donahue sexually abused him over four decades earlier as a 12 year-old boy in 1976. The man claimed that "Donahue's abuse led to decades of rage, alcoholism and drug use," and he "had trouble holding down work and had run-ins with the police from an early age." Most notably, the accuser also claimed to have since battled cancer three different times.[1]

Fr. Donahue vehemently denied the claim. A thorough investigation determined that the accuser's sex abuse claim could not have happened, and Donahue's case was deemed "unsubstantiated." Yet a compensation program set up by the archdiocese somehow concluded that the man had "suffered physical injuries and emotional injuries as a result of physical abuse" and ordered the Church to pay him $73,000.[2]

How could this be? Well, the Church had little choice. The accuser was represented by the high-profile contingency lawyer Mitchell Garabedian (depicted in the 2015 movie *Spotlight*), and a public trial for such a case would be almost impossible to win. Garabedian would have sprinted to the media with his story of a sympathetic accuser, a man who has bravely fought cancer, and the media would have taken care of the rest. One can imagine the headlines:

- "No mercy: Catholic Church fights cancer survivor over past abuse";
- "Cancer patient forced to fight another battle: Against the Catholic Church";
- "Catholic Church forces cancer patient to revisit his abuse by a priest."

No matter the facts of the case, people will often assess a case emotionally. And with the burden of proof so low, there is little the Church can do but open its wallets when it is sued.

This is yet another reality that we will never read about in the media.

Indeed, extracting money from the Church is easy. The Archdiocese of New York openly admitted to *The New Yorker* magazine in 2019 that it has "lenient standards of evidence" when giving out money to plaintiffs. It conceded that it had paid out on many "weak claims" when it came to doling out some $61+ million from a fund designated for abuse victims. The archdiocese explained that it pays out on these weak claims "in order to lead to a collective sense of resolution," though it is not entirely clear how a priest who was falsely accused could feel a "sense of resolution."[3] (This harsh reality brings to mind the case of New York's Bishop John J. Jenik.[4])

And New York is not alone. The Diocese of Houma-Thibodaux, a small diocese in Louisiana, once openly acknowledged that even though "there has not been a case that we deemed to be true," it had paid out at least one financial settlement for a claim alleging abuse decades earlier.[5]

Simply put: Fraudsters, flimflammers, and troubled individuals are scoring big cash settlements for themselves by making claims of past abuse. And the sad reality is that the more the Church pays out on these bogus claims, the more claims it gets. It all makes sense. Why not file suit? There is nothing to lose.

FAST FACT: When a contingency lawyer holds a press conference and gathers the media to announce a lawsuit against the Church, the diocese is often hearing of the lawsuit for the first time just as the public is. In fact, the lawsuit may not even have been filed in court yet.

This is a common tactic by Church-suing attorneys. The diocese has not even seen the lawsuit and is thus unable to compose a response to the media by the time the evening news is aired. The diocese is left with little to say except that it has "not yet seen the lawsuit" but it "abhors every instance of abuse."[6]

Such a milquetoast response from the diocese is exactly what the plaintiff's attorney wants all along. The immediate impression that the public gets is that the priest is guilty because that's the only side that people have heard.

NOTES

[1] Lexi Churchill, Ellis Simani and Topher Sanders, "Catholic Leaders Promised Transparency About Child Abuse. They Haven't Delivered," ProPublica, January 28, 2020. Accessed from https://www.propublica.org/article/catholic-leaders-promised-transparency-about-child-abuse-they-havent-delivered , April 2020.
[2] Ibid.
[3] Paul Elie, "What Do Church Victims Deserve?" *The New Yorker*, April `15, 2019 issue.
[4] The case involving Bishop John J. Jenik in the Archdiocese of New York was a grave injustice. Bishop Jenik was indeed falsely accused, yet his case was deemed "substantiated" by the archdiocese. For more, see TheMediaReport.com, "Braving the Cold and Heavy Rain, Bronx Parishioners March In Support of Bishop Jenik As Evidence Mounts of False Accusation," November 12, 2018.
[5] Billy Gunn and Richard Burgess, "Dioceses differ on allegation actions," *The Acadiana Advocate* (Louisiana), September 10, 2014.
[6] Some examples include: David Tarrant, "Lawsuit says Dallas diocese did not protect young girl from priest's abuse," *The Dallas Morning News*, January 31, 2020; Christian Boone, "EXCLUSIVE: New lawsuit alleges sexual abuse by longtime Georgia priest," *The Atlanta Journal Constitution*, December 20, 2018;

13

A Priest Fights Back

Fighting back in a court of law against a false accusation requires an immense amount of legal and investigative resources, resources that the vast majority of priests would be unable to afford without significant assistance from friends and supporters.

But one priest who successfully endured the long and hard road to fight back against false accusations against him was Rev. Xiu Hui "Joseph" Jiang, a priest from the Archdiocese of St. Louis.

In 2014, local media in St. Louis went wild reporting that a young boy accused Fr. Jiang of abusing him. The accusation was that Jiang somehow pulled the accuser "out of line" *during Mass* and sodomized him at least twice. But after a lengthy investigation, a 2015 lawsuit revealed the truth about what this was all about:

> "The accusations were brought by a deeply troubled and unreliable 12-year-old boy at the suggestion of his abusive father. The alleged victim had made previous unfounded allegations of sexual abuse, and his parents had a history of making unfounded claims against the Catholic Church for

monetary gain. Even a cursory investigation would have demonstrated that the accusations were impossible and that the alleged incidents of abuse simply did not happen."[1]

In addition, the boy's fourth-grade teacher not only stated that it was "virtually impossible" for Fr. Jiang to have pulled the boy out of Mass but also added that the boy was a "serial exaggerator to the point of being 'delusional'." In fact, the boy never even had any personal interaction with Fr. Jiang at all, and he "could not even identify Fr. [Jiang's] name when he made the allegation."[2]

Further scrutiny also uncovered why the young accuser was so "deeply troubled and unreliable." It turned out that his father was quite a disturbed man himself. When Fr. Jiang and his lawyers tried to serve court papers on the guy, they soon found out that they weren't the only people looking for him. The man had racked up 2 liens and 16 court judgments against him. He had also previously physically assaulted and choked the principal at the boy's school.[3]

The accuser's father wasn't found at the address listed for him publicly, his residence appeared vacated, and by all appearances he was on the run to evade service.

Thankfully, although it took longer than it should have, law enforcement cleared Fr. Jiang. But even after being exonerated, the activist group SNAP – Survivors Network of those Abused by Priests, an aggressive lawyer-funded "advocacy group" (more on SNAP in the next chapter) – continued a relentless attack on the innocent priest. In statements in television interviews, newspaper articles, letters to the editor, press releases, and on the SNAP website, SNAP leaders repeatedly identified Jiang as a "child molesting cleric" and "cunning predator" who "will molest again" and might "flee overseas like hundreds of other predator priests have done."[4]

And for merely defending himself, SNAP also claimed that Jiang had somehow "exploited legal loopholes and used legal maneuvers to escape consequences for his hurtful and illegal misdeeds."

Fr. Jiang fought back against SNAP and sued the group for defamation, including its director David Clohessy and agent Barbara Dorris.

Throughout the legal process, SNAP repeatedly defied a federal judge's orders to hand over important documentary evidence in the case. Eventually, in 2016, U.S. District Court Judge Carol E. Jackson decided she would have no more of SNAP's defiance and issued a ruling in which she plastered SNAP, Clohessy, and Dorris: "SNAP defendants' refusal to comply with the Court's discovery orders has been willful and in bad faith." But, most importantly, Judge Jackson added:

> "SNAP defendants' public statements about plaintiff (Fr. Jiang) were false and they did not conduct any inquiry into the truth or falsity of these public statements, but instead made these statements negligently and with reckless disregard for the truth."[5]

The judge also ordered SNAP to reimburse Jiang's legal fees totaling $25,100.[6]

Fr. Jiang was victorious at every level. Law enforcement cleared him, and a judge ruled that SNAP had defamed him.

THE GREATEST FRAUD NEVER TOLD

Victorious: Rev. Xiu Hui "Joseph" Jiang of the Archdiocese of St. Louis sued the activist group SNAP for defamation and won.

NOTES

[1] Case No. 4:15-cv-01008, United States District Court, Eastern District of Missouri, Rev. Xiu Hui "Joseph" Jiang v. Survivors Network of those Abused by Priests, David Clohessy, Barbara Dorris, (and more), Filing of November 9, 2015.

[2] Ibid.

[3] Ibid.

[4] Ibid.

[5] Case No. 4:15-cv-01008, August 22, 2016.

[6] Robert Patrick, "St. Louis priest settles part of civil case against accuser and clergy abuse survivor's group," *St. Louis Post-Dispatch*, October 10, 2017.

14

SNAP Uncovered

A woman named Barbara Blaine founded SNAP in 1988. A few years later, David Clohessy, an organizer with the radical activist group ACORN (Association of Community Organizations for Reform Now)[1], joined Blaine as a director on the national level.

When Judge Jackson ruled that SNAP had defamed Fr. Jiang "negligently and with reckless disregard for the truth," she unwittingly characterized how the group has acted since its inception.

Ideally, Church officials and SNAP would be collaborating together for the interests of those who were so seriously violated by priests. Unfortunately, SNAP's relentless maliciousness and hatred for the Church has made such a partnership an impossibility.

Indeed, there was a time when some Church officials thought it would be beneficial and charitable to interact with SNAP. Unfortunately, they only learned the hard way that such gestures were fruitless. One Church leader who once thought that it would be productive to reach out to SNAP was Archbishop Timothy Dolan. When he led the Archdiocese of Milwaukee, he believed that making himself available to the group would be a constructive expression of support to abuse victims.

Dolan soon learned that such an overture was a mistake. At a contentious visit to a parish in Milwaukee, a member of SNAP spat in the archbishop's face. The member then roared that he would not be silent "until there was a 'going out of business' sign in front of every Catholic parish, church, school and outreach center."

"That's when I knew I should have listened to those who told me that working with them would not be helpful," recalled Dolan.[2]

SNAP's everlasting legacy, however, is that it has defamed countless innocent priests and voiced innumerable falsehoods about bishops and priests. Indeed, in a January 2012 deposition, SNAP National Director David Clohessy admitted under oath that SNAP had released false information to the press.[3]

The sheer viciousness of SNAP cannot be overstated.

For example, in January 2012, SNAP's Clohessy issued a press release suggesting that Philadelphia Cardinal Anthony Bevilacqua was faking his cancer and dementia to avoid appearing in court at an upcoming clergy abuse trial. Less than 36 hours after Clohessy's callous remark, Bevilacqua passed away in his sleep from his illnesses.[4] (He was 88 years old.) Clohessy never apologized.

In ensuing years, SNAP would publish the email addresses and personal phone numbers of accused priests on its web site to incite harassment against them.[5] SNAP also sued for the right to harass and intimidate parishioners at

Sunday Mass.[6] The episodes of malice are legion.

Yet it was a blockbuster lawsuit filed in January 2017 by a former officer at SNAP that finally exposed the truth about SNAP to the world.

SNAP hired Gretchen Hammond in 2011 as director of development to oversee the group's fundraising operations and to boost cash inflow to the group. Ms. Hammond did so with great success, but the more she learned about the inner workings of SNAP, the more she came to learn that SNAP was not simply an innocent "victim advocacy group." She saw that it was a gang hellbent on shaking down the Catholic Church through a seedy web of lawyer kickback schemes, lawsuits, and bigotry.

When Ms. Hammond confronted SNAP president Barbara Blaine about her concerns about the group's questionable dealings with attorneys, the atmosphere changed immediately at SNAP for Hammond. "SNAP began taking retaliatory actions against her," according to the lawsuit, and the group soon fired her.[7]

Hammond filed a suit for wrongful termination, and her lawsuit was truly stunning. Among her suit's eye-opening statements:

- "SNAP does not focus on protecting or helping victims – it exploits them."
- "SNAP routinely accepts financial kickbacks in the form of donations. In exchange for the kickbacks, SNAP refers survivors as potential clients to attorneys, who then file lawsuits on behalf of the survivors against the Catholic Church."
- "SNAP is a commercial operation motivated by its directors' and officers' personal animus against the

Catholic Church."

- "SNAP's commercial operation is premised upon farming out abuse survivors as clients for attorneys."
- "SNAP callously disregards the real interests of victims, using them instead as props and tools as furtherance of their commercial fundraising goals."
- "SNAP would even ignore survivors that reached out to SNAP in search of assistance and counseling."
- "81.5% of SNAP's 2007 donations were donations by attorneys."[8]

Indeed, regarding SNAP's slippery dealings with attorneys, the lawsuit highlighted a November 2012 email in which, according to the lawsuit, David Clohessy "provided information regarding a survivor to the attorney for the purposes of filing a lawsuit on behalf of the survivor … [and then] asked the attorney when SNAP could expect a donation."[9]

And if there were any remaining doubt that SNAP's activities have had almost nothing to do with the protection of children and everything to do with bludgeoning the Catholic Church for what it stands for, Hammond's lawsuit showcased an email message composed by Clohessy that clarified this very thing. In a 2011 exchange with an individual contemplating suing the Catholic Church, Clohessy wrote:

> "i sure hope you DO pursue the WI [Wisconsin] bankruptcy … Every nickle (sic) they don't have is a nickle (sic) that they can't spend on defense lawyers, PR staff, gay-bashing, women-hating, contraceptive-battling, etc."[10]

The email speaks for itself. In the eyes of SNAP, suing

1212

the Catholic Church was not about justice and restitution for victims genuinely harmed by criminal clergy. It was about stripping the Church of its assets because of what it stands for on social issues.

Ms. Hammond was victorious in her suit, and she won a settlement from SNAP. Yet the settlement was not without a glaring act of hypocrisy. While SNAP had railed for years against the Catholic Church for arranging "secret settlements" with accusers, SNAP apparently did the very same thing with Ms. Hammond, as it was reported that "Hammond said the terms of the settlement prevented her from commenting" when she was asked by a reporter about her victory.[11]

Busting the "less than two percent" falsehood

It must be repeated that any false abuse accusation is a profound insult to genuine victims of sex abuse. With that said, it is clear that professional victims' groups and their lawyers do not like to broach the subject of false accusations.

In the rare moments that they do address the subject, they try to deny that there are many cases of false accusations by claiming that "even the Church's own data" reveals that "less than 2 percent" of accusations are false.

But this claim is simply untrue.

Indeed, a section of the 2004 John Jay Report – which surveyed accusations from 1950 until 2002 and is now many years old and stale – reported that there were 5,681 cases in which a "definitive result" was made following an investigation. 80% of the cases were deemed "substantiated"; 18% "unsubstantiated"; and 1.5% were labeled as "false."

THE GREATEST FRAUD NEVER TOLD

But wait. Annual reports have defined "unsubstantiated" as describing "an allegation for which an investigation is complete and the allegation has been deemed **not credible/false** based upon the evidence gathered through the investigation."

So, what's the difference between "unsubstantiated" and "false"? It's an important question, and it's a distinction that even the John Jay Report itself does not make very clear. What one diocese may have called "unsubstantiated" another diocese may easily have called "false."

When both the "unsubstantiated" and "false" claims are added together, **the sum of false accusations is 19.5%**, far more than the 1.5%, or the "less than 2 percent," cited by the likes of SNAP.

And that's not all. That 19.5% only covers the 5,681 cases in which a "definitive result" was made. In fact, the report recorded a total of 10,667 allegations.[12] That means in nearly half of all cases, an investigation *was never even completed or conducted*. And whereas the vast majority of uninvestigated claims involve allegations against long-dead priests from many decades earlier, surely many of these allegations are phony.

NOTES

[1] Clohessy served for nearly a decade with the Missouri chapter of ACORN. See the blog of Wade Rathke, founder of ACORN, praising Clohessy: "Blaming the Victims: Catholic Church Attack on SNAP & Dave Clohessy," March 13, 2012,

https://chieforganizer.org/2012/03/13/blaming-the-victims-catholic-church-attack-on-snap-dave-clohessy/

[2] Serge F. Kovaleski, "Complex Struggle: Prelate's Record in Abuse Crisis," *The New York Times*, May 17, 2010, p. A1.

[3] TheMediaReport.com, "*EXCLUSIVE* Deposition of SNAP's Clohessy Revealed! Clohessy Evades Questions and Subverts Court Order While Lawyers Shred Clohessy's Defense That SNAP is a 'Rape Crisis Center'," March 1, 2012.

[4] TheMediaReport.com, "Hours Before Cardinal Bevilacqua Passed Away, SNAP's Clohessy Suggested the Cleric Was Faking His Illnesses," February 1, 2012.

[5] TheMediaReport.com, "Disgrace: SNAP Now Publishes Phone Numbers and Email Addresses of Accused Clerics to Incite Harassment of Priests," December 9, 2013.

[6] TheMediaReport.com, "SNAP Wins Its Appeal To Harass and Intimidate Parishioners at Sunday Mass," March 15, 2015.

[7] *Gretchen Rachel Hammond vs. Survivors Network of those Abused by Priests* (lawsuit), In the Circuit Court of Cook County, Illinois, filed January 17, 2017.

[8] Ibid.

[9] Ibid.

[10] Ibid.

[11] Eric Berger, "Lawsuit settled, former SNAP director returns to the fight against abuse," *The Salt Lake Tribune*, September 28, 2018.

[12] United States Conference of Catholic Bishops, Washington, D.C., John Jay College study, "The Nature and Scope of the Problem of Sexual Abuse of Minors by Catholic Priests and Deacons in the United States 1950-2002" (June 2004).

15

Other Phony Attacks on the Church

It has not been only with the abuse story that the media has been reckless in its reporting. While fulfilling its zeal to attack the Catholic Church, the media has also propagated a number of other false narratives which the public has come to believe as true. For example:

The Magdalene Laundries

It has become a common belief that the Magdalene Laundries – institutions in Ireland that operated for centuries by the Catholic Church for troubled young women – were warehouses of unspeakable cruelty that only exacerbated girls' suffering. Popular movies such as 2002's *The Magdalene Sisters* – produced by the notorious Hollywood filmmaker Harvey Weinstein – popularized the notion across the globe that the laundries were crooked establishments operated by sadistic and mean-spirited nuns.

But in early 2013 – in an episode that received almost no media attention – the Irish government released the

McAleese Report, which had sought to examine the country's role in the laundries. (The chairman of the report was Irish Senator Martin McAleese.) The report contained some stunning findings, essentially revealing that the media's characterization of the laundries was a complete fiction.

Of the many scores of women who were interviewed for the government report, exactly *zero* reported being sexually abused by a nun. None. And the vast majority reported that they had never been physically punished at all.

Even the authors of the report admitted they were taken aback by "the number of women who spoke positively about the nuns." The report quoted from several women who actually lived in the laundries, and one woman in particular had something quite remarkable to say about the popular negative portrayal of the laundries in the media. She told the McAleese Commission:

> "It has shocked me to read in papers that we were beat and our heads shaved and that we were badly treated by the nuns … I was not touched by any nun and I never saw anyone touched."[1]

As for women who once appeared on television shows and other media outlets claiming that they had experienced unspeakable barbarity and unrivaled cruelty from the nuns at the laundries, it turns out that a number of them were *never even enrolled* in them.

One such woman was Kathy O'Beirne. In 2005, O'Beirne released her book, *Kathy's Story: The True Story of a Childhood Hell Inside the Magdalen Laundries*,[2] in which she described atrocious and persistent abuse with frightening detail. O'Beirne described how the nuns at the laundries pounded her so relentlessly that one particular beating actually broke her pelvis. She also claimed that a priest raped her at age 13, which resulted in her giving birth to a daughter, whom she said died 10 years later.

O'Beirne's book was a monumental success, reaching number three on the UK's best-seller list and selling nearly 400,000 copies. Reviewers raved. The *Irish Independent* heralded the tome as "a devastating account of a childhood stolen by the twin evils of child abuse and an unholy church-state alliance."[3] *She* magazine proclaimed, "Her story is so horrific, it's almost unbelievable."[4]

Well, as it turned out, the reason that *Kathy's Story* seemed "almost unbelievable" is simple: She made the whole thing up.

In September 2006, nearly a year after Kathy O'Beirne became a bestselling author, five of Kathy's brothers and sisters came forward publicly to address the media. They declared that their sister's book was a "hoax publication."[5] The siblings assured the public, "Our sister was not in a Magdalene laundry or Magdalene home."[6] With the exception of a six-week period at a home for troubled children, Kathy O'Beirne attended regular public schools.[7]

Indeed, The Sisters of Our Lady of Charity, who meticulously maintained their records, had no entry at all of the author ever being enrolled in a Magdalene facility.

As for O'Beirne's claim that she gave birth at age 14, Mary O'Beirne, one of Kathy's younger sisters, said, "Until this book came out, she never once mentioned it."[8]

"There was never any mention of it in our household as we were growing up," the sister added. "There is no birth or death certificate. There is no child."[9] Indeed, Kathy O'Beirne has never provided any documentation that she has ever given birth to anyone.

Priests never raped O'Beirne. A priest did not impregnate her.

"Our sister has a self-admitted psychiatric and criminal history, and her perception of reality has always been flawed," continued Mary. "We can understand that many people will now feel hurt and conned. Kathy is lying about all this, just like she has lied about things all her life. She is very convincing, though, and that is what makes her so dangerous."[10]

"Kathy has no credibility," Eamonn O'Beirne, one of Kathy's brothers, added.[11]

Indeed, O'Beirne's co-author, a man by the name of Michael Sheridan, later admitted that the book's claims were completely unsupported.

"I'll tell you the evidence we have," said Sheridan. "There are no documents. Those documents are either falsified or destroyed. There is no evidence or records of Kathy in the two Magdalene laundries. There never was."[12]

Pure Fiction: Hollywood's 2002 film The Magdalene Laundries *helped to popularize the belief that Ireland's facilities for troubled young women were actually warehouses of brutality. Yet a 2013 government report revealed that such a portrayal was purely mythical.*

The Keepers on Netflix (2017)

The 1969 unsolved disappearance and murder of a Baltimore nun, Sister Catherine Cesnik, certainly had all the makings of a compelling whodunnit. "Who killed Sister Cathy?" was the trailer to *The Keepers*, a multi-part "documentary" about the case that aired on Netflix in 2017.

Unfortunately, anyone looking for an honest and clear-thinking analysis of this case was unable to find it. Viewers were left with little but an unfocused scavenger hunt trafficking in speculation, innuendo, rumor, discredited science, and a healthy heap of anti-Catholic bigotry.

The central thesis of *The Keepers* was that an alleged abusive priest, the deceased Rev. Joseph Maskell, could be tied to the disappearance and murder of Sr. Cathy. Rev. Maskell vehemently denied any involvement in Sr. Cathy's disappearance before his death in 2001.

Two days before *The Keepers* was to first air on Netflix, the producers of the series received some really bad news: The body of Fr. Maskell had been exhumed months earlier, and police announced that DNA connected to the murder scene of Sr. Cesnik did not match that of the deceased priest.

Needless to say, this piece of inconvenient news put a big damper on Netflix's story. It also refuted a central accuser's bizarre tale about Fr. Maskell once showing her Sr. Cathy's corpse in a wooded area.

That central accuser in *The Keepers* was a woman named Jean Wehner, and it turned out that all of Wehner's claims of abuse surfaced through the dangerous and discredited practice of "repressed memory therapy."

The producers bent over backwards to try and legitimize repressed memory theory, but in truth, it cannot be overstated how untrue and fraudulent the practice truly is. As

THE GREATEST FRAUD NEVER TOLD

Dr. Richard J. McNally, Professor and Director of Clinical Training in the Department of Psychology at Harvard University, has written:

> "The notion that traumatic events can be repressed and later recovered is the most pernicious bit of folklore ever to infect psychology and psychiatry. It has provided the theoretical basis for 'recovered memory therapy' — the worst catastrophe to befall the mental health field since the lobotomy era."[13]

And Dr. James McGaugh from the University of California, Irvine, whose expertise in the area of memory was once profiled on CBS' *60 Minutes* program, has added:

> "I go on science, not fads. And there's absolutely no proof that it can happen. Zero. None. Niente. Nada. All my research says that strong emotional experiences leave emotionally strong memories. Being sexually molested would certainly qualify."[14]

Repressed memory therapy is indeed junk science. And it turns out that, according to court documents, Wehner has not just claimed that Rev. Maskell abused her. Wehner has also claimed abuse by:
- four additional priests;
- three or four religious brothers;
- three lay teachers;
- a police officer;
- a local politician;
- an uncle; and
- two nuns.[15]

Indeed, this topic is one that must be approached with caution and sensitivity. Not all clergy abuse victims invoke "repressed memory." The memory of actual awful abuse is all too real and devastating. But Netflix's entire series was almost completely based on the claims of what appears to be a very troubled individual.

The whole bumbling series was unfortunate, because Sr. Cesnik deserved much, much more.

Babies in a septic tank?

In June of 2014, international media erupted with the alarming story that a historian had uncovered 800 babies "dumped" in a septic tank behind a mother-and-baby home once operated decades earlier by the Catholic Church in Tuam, Ireland.

The *Washington Post* trumpeted the headline, "Bodies of 800 babies, long-dead, found in septic tank at former Irish home for unwed mothers." Boston.com – operated by the *Boston Globe* – carried the headline, "Galway historian finds 800 babies in septic tank grave" and then began its story: "Hundreds of skeletons were reportedly found inside a septic tank grave next to an area in western Ireland where a 'mother-and-baby home' once stood."[16]

For the next five years, media outlets around the world repeatedly trumpeted the story to spotlight the alleged "cruelty" of the Catholic Church.

In the end, however, the story was completely false.

The story began when an Irish resident named Catherine Corless sought to learn more about the history of St. Mary's Mother and Baby Home, which was located near where she grew up as a child. The home ceased operations in 1961, and Corliss unearthed records showing that the nuns had registered 796 deaths in the home during the decades that it operated. Corless also found out that in 1975, a pair of boys playing on the grounds of the then-closed home had come across "maybe 15 to 20 small skeletons" after smashing through a concrete covering in the ground of what *appeared* to be a septic tank. The two stories were merged together in a Facebook post, and – *voilà* – the story of "800 bodies in a septic tank" was born.[17] Yet as British writer Brendan O'Neill explained:

> "On almost every level, the news reports in respectable media outlets around the world were plain wrong. Most importantly, the constantly repeated line about the bodies of 800 babies having been found was pure mythmaking. The bodies of 800 babies had not been found, in the septic tank or anywhere else. Rather, Corless had speculated in her research that the 796 children who died at the home had been buried in unmarked plots (common practice for illegitimate children in Ireland in the early to mid-twentieth century) and that some might have been put in the tank in which two boys in 1975 saw human remains."[18]

Indeed, five years after media across the world fomented anger against the Catholic Church for "dumping 800 babies in a septic tank," an independent commission issued an interim report "in the light of a great deal of inaccurate commentary about the Tuam site." The report asserted that "human remains found by the Commission are **not in a sewage tank**."[19]

And whereas the original story of barbaric cruelty perpetrated by Catholic nuns received widespread media attention across the globe on television and on the Internet, the news of the truth received almost no attention whatsoever.[20]

The entire episode was a classic example of how there is almost no scrutiny whatsoever by the media when it comes to reporting outlandish claims against the Catholic Church. If Corless had claimed to have discovered 800 dead babies in a septic tank, could the media have at least inquired about *seeing a photo* of what she said she discovered?

Apparently not. The narrative alone of the "mean and callous" Catholic Church dumping dead babies in a septic tank was enough for the media to run with the story.

Pope Pius XII and the Holocaust

For over a half century, the media has propagated the malicious tale that Pope Pius XII was sympathetic to Nazi Germany during one of the world's darkest hours.

Nothing could be further from the truth.

When Pope Pius XII (Eugenio Maria Giuseppe Giovanni Pacelli), died in October of 1958, Golda Meir, the future prime minister of Israel, stated: "We share the grief of the world over the death of His Holiness Pius XII … During the ten years of Nazi terror, when our people passed through the horrors of martyrdom, the Pope raised his voice to condemn the persecutors and to commiserate with their victims."[21]

Indeed, as Nazi Germany's atrocities during World War II unfolded, Pius spoke out forcefully against the evils being perpetrated, thus prompting the *New York Times* in a December 25, 1941, editorial, to declare:

"The voice of Pius XII is a lonely voice in the silence and darkness enveloping Europe this Christmas … He is about the only ruler left on the Continent of Europe who dares to raise his voice at all … the Pope put himself squarely against Hitlerism … he left no doubt that the Nazi aims are also irreconcilable with his own conception of a Christian peace."[22]

Months later, headlines from the *New York Times* read, "Pope Is Said to Plead for Jews Listed for Removal from France" (August 6, 1942) and "Vichy Seizes Jews; Pope Pius Ignored" (August 27, 1942).

Yet Pope Pius' efforts during World War II surpassed mere words. Michael Tagliacozzo, "the foremost survivor on the October 1943 Nazi roundup of Rome's Jews" and "a survivor of the raid himself," said Pius' actions helped rescue some 80 percent of Rome's Jews from being captured. Said Tagliacozzo, "Pope Pacelli was the only one who intervened to impede the deportation of Jews on October 16, 1943, and he did very much to hide and save thousands of us."[23]

Isaac Herzog, the chief rabbi of Jerusalem, later sent a personal message to Pope Pius XII in 1944 stating: "The people of Israel will never forget what His Holiness and his illustrious delegates, inspired by the eternal principles of religion which form the very foundations of true civilization, are doing for us unfortunate brothers and sisters in the most tragic hour of our history, which is living proof of divine Providence in this world."[24]

Mordechay Lewy, formerly Israel's ambassador to the Holy See, has been quoted, "It is wrong to look for any affinity between [Pius] and the Nazis. It is also wrong to say that he didn't save Jews. Everybody who knows the history of those who were saved among Roman Jewry knows that they hid in the church."[25]

Yet shortly after Pius' death in 1958, a sinister

Communist propaganda campaign to rewrite Pius' role in World War II soon permeated the popular culture. Secularists, atheists, and other assorted anti-Catholics soon seized upon a new cudgel with which they could attack the Catholic Church over an emotional issue.[26]

This poisonous slander against Pope Pius XII and the Catholic Church continues today, propagated by network television, newspaper writers, bestselling books, and Hollywood celebrities.

NOTES

[1] *Report of the Inter-Departmental Committee to establish the facts of State involvement with the Magdalen Laundries*, Department of Justice and Equality (Ireland), 2013. Accessed in April 2020 from http://www.justice.ie/en/JELR/Pages/MagdalenRpt2013 (The spelling of the laundries has appeared historically as both "Magdalene" and "Magdalen.") (The laundries operated in Ireland from 1765 until 1996.)

[2] The book has also been published under the title, *Don't Ever Tell: A True Tale of a Childhood Destroyed by Neglect and Fear* (Mainstream Publishing, 2005/2006).

[3] This quote is on the cover of the paperback of *Kathy's Story*.

[4] This quote is on the cover of the paperback of *Don't Ever Tell*.

[5] Natalie Clarke, "Author of child abuse memoir accused of fabricating her past," *Daily Mail* (U.K.), September 22, 2006.

[6] Owen Bowcott, "Author's family deny tales of sex abuse," *The Guardian* (U.K.), September 19, 2006.

[7] Hermann Kelly, "Lies of Little Miss Misery – memoir of abused girl is a fake, says new investigation," *Daily Mail*, (UK), October 31, 2007.

[8] Clarke, September 22, 2006.

[9] Ibid.

[10] Esther Addley, "Author accused of literary fraud says: 'I am not a liar. And I am not running any more'," *The Guardian* (U.K.), September 22, 2006.

[11] Colin Coyle, "Sequel to Kathy's Story sparks new furore," *The Sunday Times* (U.K.), October 26, 2008.

[12] Hermann Kelly, "Kathy's co-writer admits a lack of facts," *The Sunday Times* (U.K.), September 24, 2006.

[13] June 3, 2005, letter by Dr. Richard J. McNally to the Honorable Ronald M. George, Chief Justice and Associate Justices of the California Supreme Court. RE: Nicole Taus vs. Elizabeth Loftus et al. (1st D.C.A. Civ No. A104689, Solano County Superior Court No. FCS02A557). Letter posted at http://themediareport.com/wp-content/uploads/2012/01/McNally-Repressed-Memory-letter-2005.pdf

[14] Meredith Maran (2010). *My Lie: A True Story of False Memory* (San Francisco: Jossey-Bass), p. 223.

[15] Accessed from the site of writer Mark Pendergrast, author of the book, *Memory Warp: How the Myth of Repressed Memory Arose and Refuses to Die*. See also: http://www.themediareport.com/2017/07/27/netflix-the-keepers-debunked/

[16] Shannon McMahon, "Galway Historian Finds 800 Babies in Septic Tank Grave," Boston.com, June 4, 2014. https://www.boston.com/news/world-news/2014/06/04/galway-historian-finds-800-babies-in-septic-tank-grave

[17] Brendan O'Neill, "The Tuam tank: another myth about evil Ireland," Spiked-online, June 9, 2014. https://www.spiked-online.com/2014/06/09/the-tuam-tank-another-myth-about-evil-ireland/

[18] Ibid.

[19] Commission of Investigation into Mother and Baby Homes and Certain Related Matters, https://www.gov.ie/en/publication/873470-commission-of-investigation-into-mother-and-baby-homes-and-certain-r/ cited by The Irish Catholic, "Tuam babies not buried in septic

tank, report confirms," April 17, 2019.
https://www.irishcatholic.com/tuam-babies-not-buried-in-septic-tank-report-confirms/

[20] Also much recommended: "Ireland's 'Mass Grave' Hysteria" by William A. Donohue of The Catholic League, June 2014, and "Irish Report on Irish Debunks Myths," The Catholic League, June 19, 2019. www.catholcleague.org .

[21] Dan Kurzman (2007). *A Special Mission: Hitler's Secret Plot to Seize the Vatican and Kidnap Pope Pius the XII*, (Cambridge, MA: Da Capo Press), p. 53. Cited in Ronald Rychlack (2010). *Hitler, the War, and the Pope* (Huntington, Indiana: Our Sunday Visitor), p. 273.

[22] "The Pope's Message" (editorial), *The New York Times*, Thursday, December 25, 1941, p. 24.

[23] Rabbi David G. Dalin (2005). *The Myth of Hitler's Pope: Pope Pius XII And His Secret War Against Nazi Germany* (Washington, D.C.: Regnery History), p. 83.

[24] Joseph Bottum and Rabbi David G. Dalin (2004). *The Pius War: Responses to the Critics of Pius XII* (Lanham, Maryland: Lexington Books), p. 22.

[25] Michael Paulson, "Israeli envoy to Vatican sees goal as harmony," *The Boston Globe*, June 21, 2009.

[26] In addition to the sources listed above, this author also recommends: Mark Riebling (2016). *Church of Spies: The Pope's Secret War Against Hitler* (New York, NY: Basic Books).

16

Injustice Down Under

The number of outlandishly false cases against innocent Catholic priests is legion, yet when it comes to one of the Church's highest-ranking clerics being falsely accused, the case of Australia's Cardinal George Pell stands on its own.

If history is recorded justly, the case of Cardinal Pell will go down as one the most egregious false persecutions by a government of an innocent religious official in history. The injustice that Australian government officials perpetrated against Pell cannot be overstated.

Cardinal Pell faced his first abuse accusation in 2002. The accuser was a career criminal named Phil Scott who came forward to claim that Pell repeatedly molested him as a 12-year-old boy over four decades earlier at a camp, in 1961. (Pell would have been only a seminarian at the time.) But to say the least, Scott had quite a life history. As writer Julia Yost reported:

"Scott has been a bookmaker, drunk driver, drug addict, drug trafficker, and violent criminal – an altar boy with a life of

127

crime ... [He's had] **thirty-nine convictions from twenty court appearances**, for offenses including but not limited to tax avoidance, substance abuse, and physical assault."[1]

Scott's stints in prison included serving three years and nine months for trafficking methamphetamine.[2] When Scott's claims against Pell made it to a courtroom, even though the atmosphere against the Catholic Church clearly worked in the accuser's favor, even a sympathetic judge could not get himself to side with the accuser. The judge observed, "There is sufficient evidence of dishonesty to demonstrate that the complainant's evidence must be scrutinized with special care."[3]

Indeed. While Scott claimed that his abuse occurred *in broad daylight* in front of several witnesses, the judge concluded:

> "Of the numerous people who were at the camp either as adult helpers (including seminarians) or as altar servers, and who have made signed statements and/or who have given evidence, none was aware of any inappropriate behavior by the respondent or any other adult."[4]

In other words, there was zero evidence that any misbehavior occurred at all. None. The judge smartly dismissed the case.

But anti-Catholic sentiment in Australia continued to swell enormously in ensuing years. Recall that Pell's first accusation was in 2002. In March of 2013, Victorian Police – a group racked by a history of scandal[5] – set up a "task force" to investigate Pell *even though there was not a single criminal complaint against him.*

Pell's attorney later observed, "It was an operation

looking for a crime and a complainant."[6]

Law enforcement soon amassed a gaggle of loons and attention-seeking psychos who had claimed that Cardinal Pell had abused them in some way. One such chap was Lyndon Monument, an admitted drug addict who had served almost a year in prison for violently assaulting a man and a woman over a drug debt. Monument, who also accused a boyhood teacher of forcing him to perform sex acts, claimed that Pell had "inappropriately touched" him in the late 1970s.

Then there was Damian Dignan, a dude with a criminal history for assault and drunk driving. Like Monument, he accused Pell of touching him inappropriately in the 1970s. Dignan said he lived alone, suffered from leukemia, and had "lost everything" due to alcohol abuse. In other words, this was a guy with nothing to lose and a lot to gain.

Law enforcement eventually decided, however, to put all their chips on the incredible claim of a man in his thirties who accused Pell of abusing him and another altar boy following a busy Sunday Mass in December 1996. The man made the stunning accusation that Pell, while draped in three layers of clerical vestments, sexually assaulted the pair in the sacristy at St. Patrick's Cathedral in Melbourne after catching the boys sipping on sacramental wine.

The accusations were absurd on every level. Like almost all priests, Pell would traditionally talk with parishioners as they left Mass. And the idea that Pell could have committed sexual assault in a sacristy, which would have been quite a busy room after a Sunday Mass, was ludicrous.[7]

Yet the most important part of all: The other altar boy, who died after a heroin overdose, denied ever being abused by Pell or anyone when asked by his mother.

Watching a videotaped interrogation of Cardinal Pell by

investigators was an astonishing sight to behold. The whole episode was insane. Pell remained remarkably composed throughout the questioning but was clearly incredulous at what he was being accused of. Sexually assaulting two altar boys after a Sunday Mass? In the sacristy?

Indeed, there were very few clear-thinking voices in the Australian media questioning the veracity of the case. Yet one who did say something was Australian politician Amanda Vanstone. In a May 2017 commentary in the *Sydney Morning Herald*, Vanstone began her piece by saying that she was "no fan of organized religion" but then wrote:

> "The media frenzy surrounding Cardinal George Pell is the lowest point in civil discourse in my lifetime. I'm 64.
>
> "What we are seeing is no better than a lynch mob from the dark ages. Some in the media think they are above the law both overseas and at home …
>
> "What we are seeing now is far worse than a simple assessment of guilt. The public arena is being used to trash a reputation and probably prevent a fair trial. Perhaps the rule of law sounds as if it's too esoteric to worry about."[8]

By the time the accusations against Pell reached a jury in 2018, the anti-Catholic atmosphere in Australia was so intense, it was almost a foregone conclusion that Pell would be found guilty, no matter what the facts were.[9] And that is exactly what happened. In December 2018, a criminal jury convicted Pell on five charges of sexual abuse.

Australian police hauled Pell off to prison, where he served *thirteen months in solitary confinement*. Pell later wrote:

"My Catholic faith sustained me, especially the understanding that my suffering need not be pointless but could be united with Christ Our Lord's. I never felt abandoned, knowing that the Lord was with me – even as I didn't understand what he was doing for most of the thirteen months."[10]

Thankfully, justice ultimately prevailed. In April 2020, Australia's highest court overturned Pell's guilty verdict.

Yet if there were any doubt as to the real motivation behind this entire ordeal, when justice for Cardinal Pell was finally rendered, Australian citizens vandalized Catholic churches with ugly graffiti and more.

Coming to a parish near you in the USA: In April 2020, after Australia's High Court overturned Cardinal Pell's conviction, anti-Catholics defaced St. Patrick's Cathedral in Melbourne.

NOTES

[1] Julia Yost, "The Case Against Cardinal Pell," *First Things*, July 3, 2017. Accessed from https://www.firstthings.com/web-exclusives/2017/07/the-case-against-cardinal-pell in April 2020.

[2] "Exonerated, not forgotten," *The Sydney Morning Herald*, October 15, 2002.

[3] Ibid.

[4] Ibid.

[5] Michael Cook, "Cardinal Pell felled by abuse claims – but are they credible?" MercatorNet.com, February 26, 2019.

[6] Emma Younger, "George Pell committal: Police accused of 'single-mindedly' pursuing charges, court told," ABC News (Australia), March 28, 2018.

[7] Ben Graham, "Andrew Bolt says Cardinal George Pell was falsely convicted of sexually abusing two boys," news.com.au, February 27, 2019. Accessed from https://www.news.com.au/national/andrew-bolt-says-cardinal-george-pell-was-fasely-convicted-of-sexually-abusing-two-boys/news-story/093735c7e28d42350460f05d0aca7b00 in April 2020.

[8] Amanda Vanstone, "I'm no fan of organised religion but George Pell's trial by media has to stop," Sydney Morning Herald, May 29, 2017. Accessed from https://www.smh.com.au/opinion/im-no-fan-of-organised-religion-but-george-pells-trial-by-media-has-to-stop-20170529-gwffft.html April 2020.

[9] Indeed, this author wrote about the Pell case in June 2017: "Will another innocent cleric be dragged off to prison for crimes he never committed? We believe so, but we hope we're wrong. The only thing for certain is that the haters of the Church will enjoy every moment of this." TheMediaReport.com, "Now This: The Media's Cardinal Pell Disinformation Campaign," June 30, 2017. http://www.themediareport.com/2017/06/30/cardinal-pell-case-facts/

[10] Cardinal George Pell, "My Time In Prison," *First Things*, August 2020.

17

Dallas Debacle?

At a June 2002 meeting in Dallas, Texas, in the midst of the media firestorm of reporting about Catholic Church sex abuse, the United States Conference of Catholic Bishops (USCCB) instituted the Charter for the Protection of Children and Young People, a set of policies for dioceses to address accusations against priests and to protect minors from future abuse. It popularly became known as "The Dallas Charter."

The Charter's main principle was that of "zero tolerance," meaning that any priest found to have a "substantiated allegation" of abuse would not only not be allowed to serve in ministry but also possibly removed from the priesthood, no matter how long ago the accusation.

For sure, bishops approved the Dallas Charter out of a desire to promote the message to the public that they were "tough on abuse." Yet as soon as the policy was put into place, many priests saw that the charter was not only antithetical to Church teaching but also ripe for injustice.

Only two years after Dallas, Cardinal Avery Dulles wrote an article challenging the wisdom of the charter. Dulles aptly noted that in November 2000, less than two years before its Dallas meeting, the USCCB issued a document called *Responsibility and Rehabilitation,* which objected to recently developed policies in the American criminal justice system such as mandatory sentencing and "three strikes and you're out."

Believing that prosecutorial practices often fail to uphold the dignity of both victim and offender, bishops at the time wrote, "We must renew our efforts to ensure that the punishment fits the crime." They also ultimately asserted, "Finally, we must welcome ex-offenders back into society as full participating members, to the extent feasible."[1]

Yet Dulles observed that bishops instituted an "extreme response" in the Dallas Charter that was completely contradictory to what they had earlier professed in their document about criminal justice. Dulles wrote:

> "The church must protect the community from harm, but it must also protect the human rights of each individual who may face an accusation. The supposed good of the totality must not override the rights of individual persons. Some of the measures adopted (in the Dallas Charter) went far beyond the protection of children from abuse. The bishops adopted the very principles that they themselves had condemned in their critique of the secular judicial system. In so doing they undermined the morale of their priests and inflicted a serious blow to the credibility of the church as a mirror of justice."[2]

Indeed, under the new policy, due process for accused priests was severely mitigated. Alleged unseemly remarks or foolhardy gestures were now treated on par with violent sexual attacks. The long-cherished standard of "innocent until proven guilty" was also thrown by the wayside.

In addition, accused priests that had successfully undergone treatment decades earlier and returned to successful ministries found themselves suddenly torn from the priesthood in a publicly embarrassing manner despite demonstrating that they were reformed and effective clerics. With regards to such cases Dulles added:

> "Forgiveness and reinstatement are appropriate when the sinner has repented and made a firm resolve of amendment, and when there is no reasonable likelihood of a relapse. The John Jay Report, published in February 2004, makes it clear that the majority of accused priests have only a single accusation against them. There is no reason to think that the protection of young people requires the removal from the ministry of elderly or mature priests who may have committed an offense in their youth but have performed many decades of exemplary service. Such action seems to reflect an attitude of vindictiveness to which the church should not yield …

> "Priests, like others, should be given due process of law. Even when it is clear that an offense has been committed, the church should not by her policies send the message that she does not care about the clerical sex offender or that she believes him to be beyond redemption. After correction offenders should be welcomed back into their order 'as full participating members, to the extent feasible'."[3]

Cardinal Dulles' words ultimately went unheeded, and fifteen years later, Msgr. Thomas G. Guarino, S.T.D., Professor of Systematic Theology at Seton Hall University, saw that the Draconian measures of the Dallas Charter continued to yield disastrous outcomes. In a 2019 article, "The Dark Side of the Dallas Charter," Msgr. Guarino noted that the Charter had not only continued to trash the concept of justice but had also inflicted deep wounds on the priesthood.[4]

Guarino noted that when dioceses executed inquiries into allegations of priestly misconduct, their investigations were often centered around "standards that trade in dangerous generalities." What is a "credible allegation," Guarino asked, except one in which a crime "*could have*" conceivably happened? An accusation could be "credible" merely for the fact that an accused priest was geographically at a parish at the same time as the accusation. And what is a "substantiated allegation"? How is an allegation from decades ago with no witnesses or evidence "substantiated" to the point that a priest is tossed from ministry forever? These are standards that resemble nothing like the more convincing evidence that is required in secular courts.

On the basis of a single accusation from 30, 40, or even 50 years ago, a priest can be removed from ministry and have his reputation destroyed forever. As Guarino explained:

"This entire process has had a devastating impact on priests – who know that they do not have the support of their ecclesiastical superiors and realize they can be deprived of their ministries, their reputations, and their livelihoods in the blink of an eye. **It is imperative that Catholic laity understand the impact the Charter's norms have had on priests.** One highly intelligent and deeply committed priest recently said to me that for the first time in his life he cannot recommend the priesthood as a vocation to young men. The chances for injustice are simply too great; lives can be ruined in a split second, on the basis of unproven allegations. Another priest, a vocation director for a large diocese, has stated that when he asks for time to address groups of priests

Dallas Debacle?

about fostering vocations in their parishes, he is often met with derision and disdain."[5]

Msgr. Guarino added that Catholic priests fully understand the element of sacrifice in the nature of the priesthood, but the specter of injustice from their own bishops is an obstacle that no priest should have to face. Those considering the priesthood are also well aware of the high risk of injustice.

To be clear, Guarino's missive was not a broadside against bishops. Secular forces have unleashed a relentless attack on the Catholic hierarchy, and it is fully understandable as to why bishops have acted the way they have in the past few decades:

> "Bishops in this country have been assailed by the state – with civil authorities regarding them as little more than co-conspirators in a massive cover-up. They are ceaselessly hounded by lawyers eager to cash in on the crisis, and by media outlets eager to embarrass the last institution to insist on gospel discipline in sexual matters. Add to these factors the anger of the Catholic laity who simply want the entire humiliating mess to disappear. **One must have sympathy for the bishops given the unrelenting attacks they face.** But it is just this assault that has tempted them to venture [] beyond the lines of solid theology."[6]

For sure, many priests have become disheartened by the fragmentation of the bishop-priest relationship. While Pope Francis says the relationship is supposed to be akin to "an older brother and a father," there are priests who see it as anything but that. A recent email to this author by a priest echoed this frustration:

137

"If bishops would simply be who they are supposed to be according to our theology & the spirituality of priesthood/bishop relationship and consistently apply pastoral practices. At the moment the bishop-priest relation is adversarial. It is corporatist, not person- or vocation-centered …

"Concepts like mercy, compassion, forgiveness, reconciliation, [and] restorative justice exist for only the laity. Bishops end up betraying their very office by not vigorously defending the innocent & the not-guilty priest. 'Making nice' w/ the media is interpreted as cowardice and only emboldens them and the tort lawyer too!"[7]

This priest is entirely correct that bishops too often try to "make nice" with a media that largely has no interest at all in giving the Catholic Church fair coverage. And bishops far too often fail to uphold the appearance of justice in their public statements after priests are accused of abuse. The pronouncement that priests are indeed "innocent until proven guilty" is frequently absent in bishops' remarks.

For example, in June 2020, a diocese announced that it was investigating four cases from decades ago involving four priests who not only denied the accusations against them but no longer even served in ministry. Yet in making the announcement of the investigations, the bishop proclaimed, "While the alleged incidents are from the past, we recognize the pain is still a deep and present reality for victim survivors of abuse and for their loved ones. We continue to pray for their healing and for their loved ones who support them."[8] Quite clearly, the bishop's talk of "victim survivors" and "healing" implied that these priests were already presumed guilty. This did not resemble fairness in the least bit.

Dallas Debacle?

One can only imagine the glee that Satan himself feels in looking at the state of the priesthood today: Priests living in constant dread of a phone call from the chancery requesting a meeting … The mere announcement of an allegation carrying the assumption of guilt and perpetual embarrassment … The adversarial relationship between bishop and priest … The constant negative portrayals of priests in the media.

These are dark days that beg for justice for priests.

NOTES

[1] Committee on Domestic Policy of the United States Conference of Catholic Bishops (USCCB), *Responsibility, Rehabilitation, and Restoration: A Catholic Perspective on Crime and Criminal Justice*, November 2000.

[2] Cardinal Avery Dulles, "Rights of Accused Priests: Toward a revision of the Dallas charter and the Essential Norms," America, June 21, 2004

[3] Ibid.

[4] Msgr. Thomas G. Guarino, "The Dark Side of the Dallas Charter," *First Things*, October 2, 2019, https://www.firstthings.com/web-exclusives/2019/10/the-dark-side-of-the-dallas-charter *highly recommended*

[5] Ibid.

[6] Ibid.

[7] Email to this author from a priest who wished to remain anonymous, Spring 2020.

[8] WHSV-TV (Harrisonburg, Virginia), "Diocese of Richmond starts review of allegations against 4 inactive priests," June 8, 2020.

18

A Call to the Gospel

The Catholic Church has been under attack numerous times since its inception, and there is no doubt that a persecution exists today. The anti-Catholic sentiment among the media, Hollywood, and politicians is pervasive, and these secular forces have used the issue of priest sex abuse as a cudgel to bludgeon the Catholic Church for what it stands for on matters such as sex, marriage, and abortion.

And while the Church's history is rife with saints who defended the Catholic Church in its most challenging times, today there are few such defenders when it comes to supporting the Church when it is unfairly maligned on the sex abuse issue. Rather, Catholic voices have found that it is far more convenient to simply take the same side as the secular media and not risk being attacked for "defending the indefensible" or "coddling pedophiles" if they dare defend an innocent bishop or priest.

In a recent episode on Twitter, this author defended a bishop in Virginia after he suspended a renegade priest who insisted in continuing to publish a misguided blog attacking his own bishop and propagating erroneous information related to the abuse scandals. When this author opined that the bishop was *right* to suspend the priest, this was one of the replies from a Twitter user to this author:

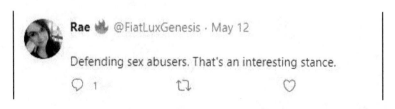

Rae 🍁 @FiatLuxGenesis · May 12

Defending sex abusers. That's an interesting stance.

Of course, this author was not "defending sex abusers" or any such thing. But the response is emblematic of the kind of nasty attack one will experience if one merely defends a bishop in any remote way when it comes to the sex abuse issue. Most Catholics would rather safeguard their eagerly amassed number of Twitter followers than risk the wrath of a mob in defending a bishop.

Indeed, by no means can wrongdoing ever be defended. The pain that genuine victims of clergy abuse have endured is all too real. But there are moral reasons why faithful Catholics should make their voices heard when priests and bishops are wrongly maligned. In the Gospel of Matthew, Jesus says:

> "'Amen, I say to you, what you did not do for one of these least ones, you did not do for me'." (Matthew 25:45b)

Are not accused Catholic priests and bishops among the "least" in today's society? What segment of our culture has been treated more maliciously and unfairly by the media for the past several decades than Catholic priests and bishops? Christians are *obligated* to act in their defense.

In the many years writing about the clergy sex abuse story, there is a photo that this author often thinks about.

Actually, it is a screenshot – a split second in a moment in time – from a June 22, 2012, television newscast in Philadelphia following the criminal trial of Msgr. William J. Lynn, who was secretary of clergy for the Archdiocese of Philadelphia. After a high-profile, 13-week trial that garnered worldwide attention, Msgr. Lynn became the highest-ranking cleric to be found guilty in a court of law over the sex abuse scandals after a criminal jury determined that Lynn was guilty of the crime of "endangering the welfare of a child."[1]

Who was the "child" that Lynn supposedly "endangered"? It was Daniel Gallagher, the very same fraudster who falsely accused Rev. Charles Engelhardt, Rev. Edward Avery, and teacher Bernard Shero of sexually assaulting him (Chapter 1 of this book). Msgr. Lynn worked with Cardinal Anthony Bevilacqua in *an archdiocesan chancery office over a dozen miles away* from the parish Gallagher attended and of course never even met or knew Gallagher. Yet a criminal jury somehow concluded that Lynn failed to "supervise" Gallagher and thus "endangered" him. Lynn's entire prosecution was indeed insane, but it worked.

Here is the screenshot:

The image is of television reporters surrounding Msgr. Lynn's sister and his nieces after they exited the courthouse after the verdict. They are clearly bewildered and devastated at the injustice that they had just witnessed over the lengthy trial. The image reveals a human dimension to the scandals that has been completely ignored.

Have Catholics forgotten that a priest is someone's son, often a brother, an uncle, a nephew, a brother-in-law, someone's friend? The humanity of our priests and bishops has been forgotten. Based only on what they viewed on the Internet or saw on TV, countless Catholics attacked Msgr. Lynn with words that are usually reserved only for serial killers and murderous dictators. Yet years later, we now know that those attacks were false and unwarranted.

Msgr. Lynn testified in court that in his position as secretary of clergy, "I felt I was helping priests and helping victims as best I could."[2] Yet Christians refused to believe him, and years later, they still feel no shame whatsoever for the harm they caused to Msgr. Lynn, his family, the Church, and to the truth.

In July 2012, after a judge sentenced Msgr. Lynn to 3-to-6 years in prison, the popular Christian blogger Rod Dreher published a post with the headline, "Monsignor Lynn To The Slammer" and wrote that Lynn and other officials like him "do not fear the justice of God, so I'm glad that they are now being made to fear the justice of the state."[3] It was a shameful thing to say about a Catholic cleric – that Lynn did "not fear the justice of God" – and it is now even more shameful now that the truth of Lynn's case has now been fully revealed. Dreher never apologized, but being a popular blogger apparently means never having to say you're sorry.

Yes, there were sins and crimes committed by bishops

and priests. Everyone knows that. But no man strives to become a priest in order to cause scandal, harm others, and bring shame upon the Church.[4] The vast majority of priests enter the priesthood because they have felt a "calling" to serve Christ and His Church. Priests administer baptisms, marriages, and funerals. They offer daily Mass and Confession. All priests surely aspire to achieve an effective and long-lasting ministry so they can ultimately be called "ambassadors for Christ" (2 Cor. 5:20).

Yet priests are not perfect; they are imperfect people. And Catholics seem to forget: In Christ's last hours before his crucifixion, two of his closest followers betrayed Him. Were the failures of Peter and Judas not a message from God Himself that His Church would sometimes be operated by men who will flounder and disappoint in spectacular ways?

Indeed, it goes without saying that many Catholics are immensely frustrated by a perceived lack of leadership from today's priests and bishops. Too many Church leaders appear to speak more passionately about left-wing political causes, such as global warming, than they do about the Sacraments and Church teaching. In an age in desperate need for voices to speak of the richness of living a God-centered life, many bishops speak more like social justice warriors rather than warriors for Christ. It seems rare when a bishop issues a statement on public policy that an atheist liberal would object to.

And when Pope Francis reportedly told a group of American bishops in January 2020 on a visit to Rome that their biggest problem was "rigid seminarians,"[5] there was a collective sense of disappointment – if not disgruntlement – from a very large body of Catholics. When bishops and faithful Catholics could have used some words of encouragement from the Holy Father, it sure seems they didn't get it.

Yet regardless of what may be an overall weak Church leadership in the United States today, there should be no excuse for the mean-spirited vitriol constantly being unleashed upon clergy.

Yes, Catholics have the *right* and the *duty* to share their opinions on important matters regarding the Church,[6] but that obligation does not include blithely attacking bishops and priests as "liars," "homopredators," and/or "Communists" – which has become common on some "Catholic" web sites and on Twitter.

Now is a time for a new call to action.

Now is a time to defend falsely accused priests and bishops.

Twitter followers will be lost, and the personal attacks for defending priests and bishops will be fierce.

But Jesus instituted the Catholic Church, and she is worth defending.

NOTES

[1] Msgr. Lynn originally was charged on *four* criminal counts. He was found not guilty on three counts and guilty on only *one*, a fact that the media almost completely ignored.

[2] Sarah Hoye, "Accused priest: 'I was helping priests and helping victims as best I could'," CNN.com, May 23, 2012.

[3] Rod Dreher, "Monsignor Lynn To The Slammer," TheAmericanConservative.com, July 24, 2012.

[4] This point is also made by the late Fr. Benedict Groeschel, CFR, in his excellent 2002 book, *From Scandal to Hope*. (Huntington, Indiana: Our Sunday Visitor).

[5] Fr. Peter M.J. Stravinskas, "Why priestly morale is in the doldrums," CatholicWorldReport.com, January 26, 2020 (highly recommended).

[6] Some Catholics invoke Canon 212 of the Code of Canon Law as justification for their attacks on Catholic leaders. Yet here is what Canon 212 actually says:

"According to the knowledge, competence, and prestige which they possess, [the Christian faithful] have the right and even at times the duty to manifest to the sacred pastors their opinion on matters which pertain to the good of the Church and to make their opinion known to the rest of the Christian faithful, without prejudice to the integrity of faith and morals, **with reverence** toward their pastors, and attentive to common advantage and the dignity of persons." (Can. 212, §3)

Index

Abraham, Lynne, 11
ACORN (activist group)
    105
Allen, Dr. Donald M., 63
Applewhite, Monica, 62
Archdiocese of Boston, 29
Archdiocese of Chicago, 2
Archdiocese of New York, 98
Associated Press, 31, 96
Avery, Edward, 6, 10, 13, 143

Benestad, Msgr. Thomas, 36-37
Bevilacqua, Cardinal Anthony,
    106, 143
Biernat, Rev. Ryszard, 85-87
Blaine, Barbara, 105, 107
Bojanowski, Matthew, 86, 87

Boston Globe, The, 63, 66, 68,
    69-71, 96
Bottlinger, James, 91-93
Boyd, Steve, 78-79, 93

Cafardi, Nicholas P., 65
Castillo, David Ramirez, 17-19
Cesnick, Sister Catherine, 117,
    118, 119
Church Militant, 52-53, 55
Cipolla, Fr. Anthony J., 44

Cipriano, Ralph, 30-31
Clohessy, David, 105, 106,
    108
Code of Canon Law, 62, 146
Corless, Catherine, 119-121
"credible" accusation, 136

"Dallas Charter," 133-136
Diocese of Buffalo, 78
Diocese of Erie, 41-43
Diocese of Houma-Thibodaux,
    98
Diocese of Pittsburgh, 43-45, 52
Dolan, Archbishop Timothy,
    106
Donahue, Fr. Richard, 96-97
Dorris, Barbara, 105, 107
Doyle, Rev. Thomas, 64
Dreher, Rod, 50-51, 144
Dulles, Cardinal Avery, 133-135
Dunn, Jack, 69-71

Eline, Paul, 5
Engelhardt, Rev. Charles, 5-10,
    13, 143

Freeman, Fr. Michael, 91, 92, 93

Gallagher, Daniel, 6-13, 30-31, 143
Garabedian, Mitchell, 97
Gauthe, Gilbert, 1, 64
Geoghan, John, 1
Goodstein, Laurie, 49
Guarino, Msgr. Thomas,
    135-137
Guglielmone, Bp. Robert E., 2

Hammond, Gretchen, 107-109
Herberger, Fr. Roy, 77, 81-82
Herzog, Isaac, 121

Jenik, Bishop John J., 98, 99n
Jiang, Rev. Xiu Hui "Joseph,"
    101-104

John Jay Report, 109-110

Kavanagh, Aoife, 22, 24
Keepers, The, 117-119
Kos, Rudy 1

Law, Cardinal Bernard, 44, 64
Lewy, Mordechay, 122
Luzzi, Salvatore, 42
Lynn, Msgr. William J., 13,
    143, 144

Magdalene Laundries, 113-116
Magdalene Sisters, The, 113, 116
Malone, Bishop Richard, 85,
    87, 88
Maskell, Rev. James, 117, 118
McGaugh, Dr. James 118
Mechanick, Stephen, 9
Mission to Prey, 21-24
Mouton, F. Ray, 64
Mueller, Rev. Joseph, 43

New Yorker, The, 98
New York Times, The, 18, 19, 96
Nessel, Dana, 56-57
Nogaro, Rev. Paul M., 82
Nussbaum, L. Martin, 61

O'Beirne, Kathy, 114-116
O'Connor, Siobhan, 87, 88
O'Neill, Brendan, 120

Paquin, Ronald, 1
Paone, Fr. Ernest C., 50-51
Parisi, Stephen, 88
Paulson, David, 42
Pell, Cardinal George, 127-131

Pennsylvania Grand Jury Report
    (2018), 33-39, 41, 45, 49, 51
Peterson, Rev. Michael, 64, 69
Pfeiffer, Sacha, 71
Philadelphia Grand Jury Report
    (2011), 5-6, 11, 12
Philadelphia Inquirer, 11, 31
Popadick, Msgr. Peter J., 82
Pope Francis, 17, 18, 21, 145
Pope Pius XII, 121-123

Quinn, David, 23-24

Rabinowitz, Dorothy, 27
Reynolds, Rev. Kevin, 21-24
Rigali, Cardinal Justin, 11
Riter, Fr. Dennis, 78, 80
Robinson, Walter, 69, 70, 71
Rossetti, Msgr. Stephen J., 67

Schiltz, Judge Patrick J., 61
Schlesinger, Arthur, Sr., 58
Scott, Phil, 127-128
Shapiro, Josh, 33-35, 41, 50
Sheridan, Michael, 116
Shero, Bernard, 6, 10, 13, 143
SNAP (Survivors Network of
    Those Abused by Priests), 11
    102-103, 105-109, 110
Sorensen, Mariana, 11-12
Specht, Charlie, 75-79, 80, 81,
    82-83, 87, 93
Spotlight, 73-75, 101
Steier, Donald, 28
Steinfels, Peter, 54
Stravinskas, Rev. Peter M.J.,
    147n
"substantiated" allegation, 136

Index

Tagliacozzo, Michael, 122
Thieman, Fred, 44
Trautman, Bishop Donald W.,
    41-43
Tuam, Ireland, 119-120

"unsubstantiated" allegation, 29-30
USCCB (United States Conference
    of Catholic Bishops), 133, 134

Vanstone, Amanda, 130
Voris, Michael, 52-53, 55

Walsh, Joseph, 10-11
Washington Post, The, 119
Wehner, Jean, 117, 118
Weinstein, Harvey, 113
Williams, Seth, 5, 11, 14n
Wuerl, Cardinal Donald, 43-45,
    50, 51, 55

Zubik, Bishop David, 45

A note from the author:
Thank you for your interest in this book.
If you found this book informative, will you consider leaving a
positive review on Amazon? It would be much appreciated.
I also invite you to visit TheMediaReport.com for more stories
related to the important issues raised in this book.

~ Also by David F. Pierre, Jr. ~

Double Standard:
Abuse Scandals and the Attack on the Catholic Church

"*Double Standard* is **essential reading** for anyone who wants to hear the other side of the clergy sexual abuse scandal ... Even for someone who has read about this subject for years, it was **eye-opening** to me."
– Thomas Peters, American Papist, CatholicVote.org

"I **highly recommend** this book."
– Gus Lloyd, The Catholic Channel, Sirius/XM Radio

Catholic Priests Falsely Accused:
The Facts, The Fraud, The Stories

"This is an important topic, and not just for priests and bishops! Everyone should be concerned about this. Please check out *Catholic Priests Falsely Accused: The Facts, The Fraud, The Stories.*"
– Rev. John T. Zuhlsdorf ("Fr. Z"), "What Does The Prayer Really Say?", wdtprs.com

"David Pierre's *Catholic Priests Falsely Accused* is an important volume ... [T]he author shows that legitimate outrage about abuse can at times boil over into wanton hysteria."
– Rev. Thomas G. Guarino, S.T.D., Professor of Systematic Theology, Seton Hall University

Sins of the Press:
The Untold Story of The Boston Globe's Reporting on
Sex Abuse in the Catholic Church

"[A] **short but powerful work** ... All Catholics – and anyone else of good will and fairness – should be most grateful for this 'tell-all' call-out of the hypocrites at the *Globe* and their fellow-travelers around the country."
– Rev. Peter M. J. Stravinskas, *The Catholic Response*

CPSIA information can be obtained
at www.ICGtesting.com
Printed in the USA
BVHW031304090921
616453BV00010B/48

9 798651 551620